TODAY IS THE VINTAGE A̶... ...passionately

cherished, it exists only because of everyone and everything that has come before it . . .

Inspired by the gossipy, tell-all tabloids of the 1950s, *Vintage Confidential: Retro Rattled, Tales Tattled—Confessions of the World's Third Oldest Profession* blows the lid off more than just your grandmother's favorite cookie jar.

Weaving memoir, personal essays, astounding true stories, and a smattering of truth-inspired fiction, nothing is "confidential" or off the table—it's all here in this sexy, sardonic, sometimes shocking vintage-themed collection of riveting tales told in technicolor prose.

Like a kingdom of kitsch, the myth of retro-obsessed America is split into a thousand cultural moments of pithy yet poignant discoveries . . . from estate sale indiscretions, monkey obsessions, cupcake confessions, octogenarian miscalculations, presidential interventions, and celebrities unshelled (Mr. Peanut, we must confess!) to terrifically fun funerals, prurient podcasts, power hoarders, and resale schnorrers gone amuck.

It's Vintage People, Places, and Things . . . Legends appear, such as Andy Warhol, Paul America, Phyllis Diller, poet Gwendolyn Brooks, milliner Raymond

Hudd, drag icon Julian Eltinge, and can't-be-named-others . . . Vintage Places That Never Were, such as the Titanic Hotel, the Chicago Spire, and Pee-wee Land . . . and Vintage Objects Lost . . . In Space or simply misplaced in our collective closets of collecting "all this stuff."

On the heels of his highly praised debut memoir *Selling Dead People's Things*, Duane Scott Cerny once again gives the reader the vintage business . . . literally. Monstrously mischievous, the laughs come as fast as the gasps while trolling the tales of "The World's Third Oldest Profession."

Like a trench-coated exhibitionist, *Vintage Confidential* invites you to look, laugh, and perhaps even lust after what's left of the retro world: the great vintage sale of the twenty-first century.

This is yesterday's future . . . today!

VINTAGE CONFIDENTIAL

Retro Rattled, Tales Tattled

Confessions of the World's Third Oldest Profession

DUANE SCOTT CERNY

Author of *Selling Dead People's Things*

Vintage Confidential:
Retro Rattled, Tales Tattled—Confessions of the World's
Third Oldest Profession

Copyright © 2022 by Duane Scott Cerny

Published by Thunderground Press
Chicago, IL

ISBN: 978-0-9998949-2-7
eISBN: 978-0-9998949-3-4

Cover and Interior Design: GKS Creative
Copyediting and Proofreading: Kim Bookless
Project Management: The Cadence Group
Cover Photo: Author's Collection

SECRETS SPILLED
ADVANCE PRAISE FOR *VINTAGE CONFIDENTIAL*

What is this book about? It ranges from screamingly funny—witty, sassy, deliciously snarky to wildly bewildering to *God, I just love spending time with Duane Scott Cerny!* And contrarily, "Retail Loses Wag; Resale Finds Swag" is a wonderfully observed essay—worthy of publication in the *New Yorker*—a serious assessment of retail and resale. The fact that it didn't make me laugh didn't dampen my interest. Go figure! I don't give a fuck about Marge and Jack or Evelyn and George, but I LOVE when Duane is in the story . . . I want to hang around him because I love his sense of humor and his way with words. I want to see things through his eyes. He makes me laugh like a crazy person! Broadly, this is a book about resale, Vintageland, but then again, some of the funniest stories don't have anything to do with that. (FYI: I loved the episode about his stint as the president of his co-op board.) I don't know what trip I've been on, but I'm always on his side!
—GRETCHEN CRYER, playwright/actor/writing coach

From basement to penthouse, Lucite to Bakelite, this read is one heck of a ride! Through hoarders, schnorrers, dreamers, and schemers, Duane Scott Cerny takes his reader on an exhilarating expedition through territory heretofore unconsidered, let alone explored. It's a zany, poignant, and unforgettable glimpse of trash, treasure, fantasy, and reality. The author's mind is as eclectic and eccentric as his subject matter, and he shares both with generous abandon.

—JULIE GOLD, Grammy Award–winning songwriter

Selling Dead People's Things is a classic book and one of a kind. If you've read it, you wanted to read more. Now Duane Scott Cerny delivers . . . *Vintage Confidential* is extra crispy, offering new excursions into the inevitable world of What They Left Behind but also more about this unique, witty, never-say-die (until they've amassed enough good stuff) entrepreneur. At times laugh-out-loud funny, other times quietly touching, it has everything—from lint, limoncello, and Lucite to Phyllis Diller, Mr. Peanut, and the Lost in Space game I'd somehow never heard of. This book is universally relevant, for, as Duane is famous for saying, everyone's an estate sale waiting to happen!

—BOZE HADLEIGH, author of *Scandals, Secrets, and Swan Songs* and *Elvis Forever*

Anyone who loves David Sedaris will want to take this HILARIOUS yet extremely personal and heart-touching ride with reluctant poet and comic memoirist Duane Scott Cerny. There are so many fascinating too-good-to-be-true stories to share within these pages: you'll travel through the bedrooms, garages, and erotic escapades of eccentric collectors and their descendants, with vivid descriptions of interiors worthy of *Architectural Digest* in some cases and *Hoarders Weekly* in others. This was a pure joy to read; the writing is so original and quippy. I was blown away by the author's previous book, *Selling Dead People's Things*, but I love *Vintage Confidential* even more and look forward to reading any and all future stories told by this delightful literary talent.

—SALLY SCHWARTZ, Randolph Street Market

Rosebud. That material thing, forgotten, or neglected, or tossed into the junk heap, but is, in fact, the concretization of the ineffable forgotten thing, the thing most tender. The ever-irrepressible Duane Scott Cerny in his marvelous new book, *Vintage Confidential*, takes us on a kaleidoscopic ride, telling juicy stories of vintage from A–Z, with detours and wicked flights of fancy. Entertaining for sure, Cerny then gives a sophisticated analysis of the how and why of the vibrancy of the vintage/resale market as retail suffers a decline. Vintage speaks to us. For me, this book at its heart is the eternal loss and

gain of human enterprise. Follow the love stories: Jane (and Duane) and the monkeys, and Evelyn's opening salvo to George regarding his jacket: "Buffalo plaid?"
— BRENDA CURRIN, actor/educator

Vintage Confidential takes a colorful, speedy whirl through dozens of offbeat stories, essays, and musings that spring from the seasoned mind of the author of *Selling Dead People's Things*—weird real-life images cobbled from decades of perusing the claptrap that presents itself to those who buy up the remains of those who no longer remain. Characters appear: Phyllis Diller, Chicago milliner Raymond Hudd, an unmarried and unnamed couple who design a high-rise private sex den for in-town assignations, Mr. Peanut, Warhol's superstar Paul America, and gender-bending silent film star Julian Eltinge, along with Magnolia Bakery cupcakes and Marie Kondo. Truly a wild ride, all in rat-a-tat prose. The author delivers rapid-fire turns of phrases that can only be described as life seen through the lens of sotto voce, and the reader is taken, like a metal ball slam dancing inside a pinball machine, through poignant personal essays about childhood and the bizarre characters met along the way in showing up to buy (and then sell) the detritus of the lives of others. Far-out fantasy interactions with unlikely characters (such as Donald Trump) help form a crazy quilt

of stories that together tell a story of life in the fast lane of the vintage dealer.
—CHIP CORDELLI, Vintage Treasure Snack

An important connection revealed itself between this reviewer and Duane Scott Cerny, author of *Vintage Confidential.* The TITANIC. No, not the ship but the greatest board game ever made. How could I put a book down by someone whose deepest desire also includes winning the Titanic board game? The bonus here is following the author on a deeply personal level while he finds his way in this wacky treasure hunt. This book is for everyone who wants to find their own niche, their own way, and thinks it can't be done. It can. It's never just about the "stuff." The people, stories, emotions, and memories are what make *Vintage Confidential* a most absorbing, if not compelling, read.
—MELISSA SANDS, dealer/promoter, Vintage Garage Chicago

In *Vintage Confidential,* best-selling author Duane Scott Cerny takes readers on an enjoyable, eclectic, episodic ride from mid-century modern to Grandmillennial style, in shades of understated gray scale and vibrant Technicolor. Throughout, Cerny serves a delicious slice of Americana pie with a little kitsch, a little pop culture, a little melancholy, and a lot of life mixed in.
—BRAD FORENZA, podcast series creator of *Around the Sun*

On the heels of his highly lauded memoir, *Selling Dead People's Things*, Duane Scott Cerny has upped the ante with his latest offering, *Vintage Confidential*. Imagine if John Waters and O. Henry somehow birthed this untamed child, creating a banquet of witty, funny, and mischievous stories, some endearing and others that will have you laughing so hard you might pee your pants. This collection of essays and tales about everyday people and personalities celebrates the more kooky and eccentric side of being human, flush with all its peculiarities. I truly recommend reading *Vintage Confidential* for its variety of vignettes that together make for a real showstopper.

—MARK CONTORNO, composer

CONTENTS

The soup of the day is the same as yesterday:
Cream of Regret.
—Anonymous

INTRODUCTION

Whether this is your first "go-round" with me or—poor devil—your second, I thought it best to give you a literary heads-up. You see, last night I saw the sequel to the remake of an encore presentation. And I wasn't even watching television. I thought I'd gone back in time . . . to when aliens ruled the planet. Last week, to be specific. Thursday to be exact. Lunchtime to be neurotic about it.

I thought I was Shirley MacLaine in another career, which I'm only mentioning because an alien or three will appear in one of the stories you're about to read. Fictional aliens, to be sure, but in a familiar setting. You'll find there's a method to my meandering madness, regardless of your planet of purported origin or the reason you picked up this book in the first place.

But I digress . . .

Always preferring to keep one's expectations low and the depths of one's frenemies even lower, I present my hybrid memoir of firsthand vintage adventures and secondhand escapades with a smattering of personal observations and essays.

So, for your enjoyment, I've prepared a number of true tales—or perhaps better/bitter tales based on true stories. Inspired by the sordid gossipmongering issues of 1950s "Confidential" magazines and similar tawdry tabloid scandal sheets, *Vintage Confidential* names the names when it can and alters them when it cannot. You're invited to play along, but I warn you that my hints often go astray, like a cat unwilling to be pawned off on a soon-to-be-ex friend.

There's sex, fame, crime, immorality, revenge—and that's just in the first fifty pages. Everyone (mostly) remains blameless, except for my self-deprecating self. So, dear reader, my only request is: No questions! I'm not answering anything short of a phone call from the dead . . . or a new agent.

As you're already quite aware, resale is not without its tightly confined spaces or the presentation of an occasional unrequested single digit. Speaking of confinement, since the publication of my last book, *Selling Dead People's Things*, many readers have asked what I've been up to—as if modifying facial recognition software to locate mid-century modern (MCM) furnishings in real estate listings doesn't keep me busy enough. Seriously.

In truth, I've been simultaneously pitching two vintage-related reality television show concepts:

1) *Scavenge: (insert city name here)*
New York City was the first proposed location where designers would scour the streets of the five boroughs in search of curbside vintage treasures and then fully furnish an overpriced cubicle-sized studio apartment in the East Village with their street-glitz finds. The bad news is that, apparently, no one in New York City wants to get dirty unless they're online naked. The worse news: *Scavenge: Gary, Indiana* would require hourly tetanus shots.

2) *Flip of Fate: The Paranormal House Renovation Show*
Amateur interior designers would compete to remodel verified haunted houses in a race to the death, mostly of sad decor. The bad news: the lack of any color other than white turned off most of the participating ghosts. The worse news: the Ku Klux Klan offered to pick up the program but only if it were broadcast on Fox.

Okay, I think we're all caught up here . . .

If you're brave enough to continue, you'll be meeting a number of characters based on actual living (or dead) persons whose names have been changed but not their exploits. Hey, I can't change other people's poor decisions. That's why God invented the red carpet and Andy Cohen. Have I apologized for everything that follows? Hardly.

But now, we have an estate sale to stalk, so get back in my creepy paneled van for our confidential trip through Vintageland. Tonight, I have to be home early—I'm catching a Shirley MacLaine film festival on TCM. I'll either see myself or, sadly, discover that reincarnation is just the repetitive use of nondairy substitutes.

CHAPTER 1

LUST AND FOUND

I'm a bit of snoop. Not that I started out that way—absolutely not. Being disturbingly shy as a child, I grew up in fear of nearly everything. One of my earliest memories is a simple one: I'm seated with my family at the dinner table, and suddenly the black rotary wall-mounted telephone begins to ring. The meal immediately stops. All of us—Mom, Dad, and sister—put down our forks in worry.

"Whoever would be calling us?" my mother asks. "And why would someone be calling us *now?*"

The phone continues to ring three times, four times, five times. My father looks at my sister, my sister to me. Inexplicably, it feels as if time stands as frozen as our dinners cool. Even the smell of my mother's gag-inducing lentil soup seems to dissipate in the air.

Six rings. Seven. Eight. Finally, it stops. *Whew!* Anguish expelled.

Think about a family too frightened to answer their own telephone at dinnertime. We lived as if we were part of some Bohemian witness relocation program, running from the law, fearful our dumplings would be confiscated by the yeast police. If only the telemarketer on the other end of the telephone had realized the panic they'd caused. Who knew a donation request for the Policeman's Benevolent Fund or a bad Florida time-share pitch could be that fear inducing? Digestion was not my childhood friend.

Today, I consider this memory whenever I'm invited into someone's home or estate to purchase their belongings. An uncomfortably shy boy has grown into a man who can panic at the opening of a door, particularly when it's not his own.

By this point in my life, it's rather a force of will to put aside the angst and tell myself, *This is what you do for a living, dummy!* Only the intoxicating promise of some great unknown or hidden vintage score breaks my own heritage of panic: the uncertain promise of a retro reckoning with my sweaty checkbook.

Now for every hundred or so estate doorways I pass through, there comes an engaging story. Engaging but not typically interesting enough to notch my notebook. But every now and hopeful then, I'll find the sweet spot:

a tale so curious, so oddly captivating that its telling—and retelling—reveals the very essence of being human and, perhaps most important, our "collecting" nature.

Bear with me as I relate a most delicate adventure in real estate. Do not be burdened with locations and identities; privacy is paramount in today's tale on a myriad of levels. Seeing may be believing, but as for tasting—well, prepare to have your mouth watered.

Together, we're standing before iconic twin residential towers of mid-century modern design: the architect's name is world-famous, and the structure is home to many of Chicago's most notable players in commerce, politics, and other profitable professions. Crane your neck skyscraper high and let your eyes focus on the majesty of these twenty-story masterpieces. Note the symmetrical perfection of glass and steel, the thousands of windows fitting together with puzzle-like exactness. We're about to experience how perfectly confounding the interior will be as well.

Entering the structure, the lobby does not disappoint. More chrome and glass, sleek MCM furnishings of reissued design, and an excellent match for the modernity of the locale. The elevators are still quick and efficient as we're pulled high into the building's interior core. Exiting, we travel down a long, plush, carpeted hallway to its end, a coveted corner unit in the sky. It is here that Robert, the estate manager, awaits us—a stylishly handsome gentleman in his sixties with both a paunch and, as we will soon discover, a punch.

Greeting us at the double-wide door, he opens it to reveal the floor-to-ceiling decorative nature of the apartment, with a mirrored entryway reflecting us in every direction. Look up, look down, because you're mostly everywhere.

"I don't ever recall seeing a mirrored *floor* before," I offer, and Robert is quick with his three-word response: "Oh, just wait!"

Immediately to our right is a heavily fabricated clear Lucite entry table, its curves prophetically sexy and slanted against a mirrored backdrop. A small pair of Lucite lamps flank either side of the table, their sharply focused chrome shades similarly reflective. But this is mere decorative foreplay before we discover the exacting designer detail of every object, if not moment, to follow.

Upon entering the huge two-bedroom corner unit in one of the most iconic MCM residences of the city, we find that nearly all the non-load-bearing walls have been removed, blown away, gone. In its place remain nearly two thousand square feet of wide-open space and the endless sky views that the heavenlike windows now offer.

A sleek, modern kitchen is built into a small portion of one wall, an island with a pair of Lucite stools before it. Two small doorways flank the giant room, each leading to mirrored hallways and matching over-the-top "his and hers" bathrooms. "His" features luxurious Calacatta squares of a black-and-white patterned marble, while "hers" embraces pink and white. Nearly every detail in these pampered Pompeii-like rooms births an air of unparalleled luxury, the cost of such remodel seemingly unimportant to the creator's hand. Or speaking bluntly: if you have to ask the price of the bidet, you can't splash in it.

Our eyes return to the spectacular main room, where it is critical to note again that even though all the bedroom walls have been removed, the bedrooms remain intact . . . well, mostly. To the far end of this expansive studio are three marble stairs, delivering you to a large round cobalt-blue jacuzzi, its reflection a mirrored mimicking in oval above. The hardware, fabricated in the foundry of New York's P. E. Guerin, of course, spout with expense, providing a decadent mini-Niagara of a waterfall for the half dozen or so lucky luxuriants of this shrine to watersports.

At the opposite side of the apartment is a similarly elevated surround of stepped marble, but here the center of attention is an enormous round bed of similar proportion to the jacuzzi. It is equally beautiful with a crisp gray silk bedspread and matching sheets and pillows. Identically mirrored in the ceiling, the bed beckons to dream the sleep of angels—especially if you'd tired from your demon lovemaking from prior playful hours.

Perhaps we should now take a breathtaking pause and consider the lusty view we've experienced in more lurid detail: a sizable two-bedroom apartment has been remodeled into one giant playroom. The effect, we should so ponderously pander, rather puts the "stud" in studio. Who could create such a prurient palace of mirrors, water, and Lucite?

It is at this point we have to remind ourselves that today we're here to buy some furniture, and not just drool. And that is how Robert, our teasing estate manager, comes into play. "You're not going to believe these pieces," he offers. "Check this out!" From the pocket of his sports coat, Robert pulls out a large remote control and pushes a button. Like a trick from a Las Vegas showroom, the magic is about to start.

Before us sits a uniquely oversized rectangular coffee table—Lucite, of course. Yet now, slowly, silently, it begins to rise to full dining table height and use. *Yup, wow!*

Our host, one can easily note, loves to demonstrate. "Custom-made," he boasts, pushing the button once more as it gracefully lowers back to coffee-table height. "I have the original receipt: fabricated in 1988 for eighty-five hundred dollars."

Now Robert moves to the only column in the apartment—a round, white, highly polished pillar in the center of the great room. Out of another pocket, he procures a second remote control and pushes the button; the column begins to dramatically open, vertically splitting itself into two huge sections, revealing the most spectacularly tricked-out cocktail bar our widening eyes have ever seen. *Wow 2.0!*

Robert waives another piece of paper in our direction. "I have the original receipt for this as well, custom made for twelve thousand dollars in 1988. In fact, the entire apartment was remodeled in the late '80s and has remained untouched since then. Crazy, right? Everything is so . . . pristine, modern even. It's all rather, well, timeless."

And, of course, he's right. The interior space is not so much a time capsule as a time traveler; the furnishings of the apartment now almost hauntingly back in fashion. It is as if the mind behind this apartment and its contents somehow morphed the Playboy Club aesthetic of the 1960s into the sexy retro stylings of the 1980s.

Robert hands us the remote controls and, like kids in an adult toy store, we repeatedly push the buttons, squealing in delight. Up and down. Up and down. Open, close. Open, close. Oh, nothing subliminal here, right?

However, it's now time to push Robert's buttons.

I sit back on a velvet-upholstered Lucite love seat. It's now my turn to begin my begging.

"Robert, Robert, Robert. Please tell us the story. An apartment like this—the opulence, the detailing, the furnishings—the sheer sexiness of this space, not to mention the expense! Please, tell us what you know . . . how?"

Robert plops himself down on one of a pair of thick Lucite chairs—and you, please take the other. Trust me, it'll be worth your stay.

"Well," he begins with a roll of his eyes and a tongue to follow, "I've been schmoozing with the doorman and doorwomen on this particular matter. In buildings like this—expensive condos or co-ops where famous, if not infamous, people reside—the only ones who know what's *really* going on with the rather complicated comings and goings of residents, visitors, and deliveries are the door people.

"I've only been representing this estate for a few months—the individual who inherited it is unnamed for privacy reasons—and they've been sitting on it for decades. Other than the cleaning lady and a few maintenance people, no one's been in here for ages."

I stutter out: "You hear about places like this—well, not like *this* exactly—but apartments left abandoned yet still financed and maintained, taxes paid, etc. How?"

Robert relaxes and releases a similar sigh. "In this particular case, I have to say it rather makes sense. You see, all the details, the mirrors and Lucite and luxury that oozes from every conceptual corner of this unit were designed by a couple. Two people, not one."

I hear the air escaping from your mouth as well. And now we're both thinking, *Kinky,* except I say it out loud.

"Yes and no. I mean, not exactly," Robert corrects with a shake of his head and a wave of a finger. "Not a couple in the traditional sense of the word. And not a husband and wife either. I've talked to the door people who worked here back in the day when this unit was first remodeled. The entire apartment was created by partners in a small local design firm. A man and a woman. Actually, being sexually-oriented accurate, a gay man and a straight woman."

Is your brow furrowing yet? Mine is.

Robert is reveling in this revelation. "This was their city apartment. Each had their own private residences outside of the city, but when either one was in town, this is where they lived and, well, played. Rather a Lucite love nest, as it were."

Are you still with me? I'm still trying to catch up.

"It seems," Robert continues breathlessly in a full gossip gallop, "that she had her boyfriends, and he had his as well. That was the purpose of this apartment, a residence of sexual convenience and comfort. Why not have it be extreme, luxurious, and over-the-top seductive? Why not indulge one's wants in the most lavish way possible?"

Not being a smoker, I still suddenly have the urge to light up one in imagined postcoital bliss. We sit for a relaxing moment, pondering in the afterglow of this voyeuristic—if not nosy—news. It's both sexy and somewhat sad, but what is left behind is still stunning, and the story is equally mind-blowing.

Robert stands, and I reach for my checkbook. "So that's the story," he concludes. "But now it's time for what all estates eventually must do: settle. Time had to pass, as did the creative pair who imagined this place into reality."

Reality. I consider the word as I take a last glance about this amorous wonderland and see our still-shocked reflections in a nearby mirror.

Oh, yes. Reality. Here we are today.

CHAPTER 2

THE GARBAGE CAN KIDS

Today I find myself in a cramped space underneath the basement stairs of a home in a near northwest suburb of Chicago. I must confess, it's not the first time I've found myself so dug in to trouble, nor will it be my last.

Stacked high to the above descending steps are more than one hundred board games of every description, all from the 1960s and '70s, nothing more contemporary. Gratefully, the basement is dry, and the games are near-mint wonderful. Not the most salable of things—Monopoly, Clue, Operation, Twister, etc., but there are also a few scarcer games: Lost in Space, The Partridge Family, The Munsters, and my personal childhood favorite, The Sinking of the Titanic. Yes, one has to save oneself and fellow passengers because with each toss of the dice, a detailed die-cut representation of the ship slips further beneath the waves. Bad taste, just terrible, but great fun to a ten-year-old.

I am handing off each rescued game to a middle-aged man standing just beside the basement staircase. His name is Jimmy, and he's in his forties with the beginning of a gut and the ending of most of his hair. His brother, Tom, is helping my partner, Jeff, sort through Japanese stainless flatware and assorted kitchen kitsch, such as Bakelite utensils, early kitchen gadgets, wondrous whisks, spectacular spatulas, and enough jadeite to satisfy the most jaded of cooks. In short, both Jeff and I are in our element.

Pleasantly, Jimmy reminisces with the handing off of each collectible and doesn't slow down the process with memories too rich to allow resale. "Oh, I loved Twister," he exclaims. "Of course, the last time we played, my brother climbed on top of me to win and kicked over a hurricane table lamp. We caught hell from Mom for that one!"

"Stratego!" he continues. "Forgot about that one—kinda boring." A pause. "Family Affair? Must have been a gift from our aunt—she always wanted nieces!" And again: "Oh, Battleship! Now this was one of my favorites: 'You sunk my battleship, dorkwad!'"

"Dorkwad?" I ask, passing a still-shrink-wrapped copy of Aggravation back up to Jimmy, who laughs. I now shuffle myself out of the corner to stand upright and stretch my aging spine. "I think these games are aggravating what's left of me," I complain.

But Jimmy remains happy to relive his childhood, examining each game as if it's Christmas morning all over again. I look to his side to see that we've unearthed a huge pile of memories. It's the start of a great vintage haul.

Jimmy and I spent the better part of the morning sorting out an enormous collection of toys and collectibles from this packed but well-kept basement. We shuttle dozens of boxes up the stairs and begin to amass a pile within the confines of the attached two-car garage. There, Jeff and Tom have added to the now-rising mountain of merchandise with the assorted treasures found from the rest of their late father's home.

Though such sorting can often be difficult, the brothers address the task with almost casual efficiency, which is how Jeff and I often attack such matters. However, as the day wears on and the brothers' strength diminishes, so do their moods. Jimmy becomes less chatty, Tom less enthusiastic. Maybe these estate-sorting hours have turned into more work than they had planned. Or maybe, I somehow fear, there's something else.

By midafternoon, the four of us take a break in the garage, sucking down bottled water and reviewing the multi-foot-high pile of stuff we've unearthed. This is now the first opportunity Tom has had to see what Jimmy has removed from the basement—and the first chance for Jimmy to see what his brother has agreed to sell from the rest of the house.

Tom pushes aside a collectible game board or three, thinking. He sniffles a bit, holding back something akin to both a tear and a laugh. Emotions are funny like that—one easily morphs into the other, often without our conscious control.

"I forgot how many toys Dad gave us," he says to no one in particular. "Jesus, kind of overkill, right?"

Jimmy opens a metal box containing the remains of a well-played Erector Set. "Yeah," he agrees, "but we always knew that."

An uncomfortable silence fills the garage as the brothers lightly finger the toys while setting aside a box full of baseballs and mitts, holding up a half-naked G.I. Joe figure, and pushing a set of uncooperative Hot Wheels cars back into the slots of their vinyl garage.

Finally—and perhaps mistakenly—I break the long quiet. "Your dad," I offer, "must have really loved you guys. I mean, I've never seen so many toys in one place."

Tom sniffs again. "Oh, yeah. He was crazy generous like that. We got everything."

"Hah!" Jimmy exclaims, adding, "Everything except what we really needed."

"No," Tom snaps, "that's not fair. Dad did the best he could."

"I didn't say he didn't. But come on . . . *everything?* Seriously, man?"

Suddenly it appears a third rail has been hit and not just on a vintage train set. Jeff, sensing the tension and wanting to move the process along, begins to start an inventory of the items we're about to purchase. I step aside, now feeling a bit guilty I'd said anything at all.

Tom leans uncomfortably against the doorway leading into the house. "Um," he starts, the sound directed more at Jeff and me than to his brother. "You see, after our mom died . . . well, Dad just wasn't the same."

Jimmy gives half a snort. "I'll say. Bit of an understatement there."

"He always had control issues," Tom continues. "But our mom kept it in check. But once she was gone . . ."

"Things got nutty!" Jimmy finishes. "Our lives, the house, it all got frickin' nutty."

Trying to de-escalate the tone, I comment: "Well, this house is really organized, super clean. We've sure seen our share of disasters, but not your dad's house."

Now both brothers give a snort, finally appearing to agree on something.

Jimmy seems eager to finish my thought. "Organized? Organized chaos, more likely." He looks about the garage for a moment then moves toward a group of metal cabinets riveted to the wall. Opening the first cabinet reveals row upon row of used coffee cans, each closed tightly with a plastic lid. He tosses one of the cans to his brother with the words, "Show them!"

With a reluctant grimace, Tom slowly opens the lid and tilts its content toward us. I lean in for a closer look but can't discern what I'm seeing.

"Dryer lint," Jimmy announces. "We have almost one hundred coffee cans filled with dryer lint. I actually think our father did laundry just so he could create the lint. And that's not even the weirdest part. Before he passed, Dad told us he would hide money in the cans, but we've never found a dime."

"Actually," Tom interjects, "I found a dime once."

"Don't be a smartass, Tommy! Dad wasn't right in the head. You know that." Jimmy closes the cabinet and turns to us. "I'm not saying he wasn't a good man. He was. But he gave no thought whatsoever about us living like this."

Another pause silences the garage.

I say, "You know, guys, we've seen a lot of situations like this; actually, situations much, much worse. Your dad's house is cluttered, sure, but it still seems like it was a nice place to grow up."

Tom sets the coffee can aside. "Well, appearances can be deceiving, I guess. How do I say this? Dad gave us everything, absolutely, and he worked hard. He was a foreman at the General Electric plant here in town. But once Mom passed, the weird hoarding began. He just couldn't throw anything away."

"Like ever," Jimmy echoed. "It got so bad that . . ." He stopped and shook his head in anger. "Hey, you know how every town has a garbage night? The night you put your garbage cans out for collection?"

Jeff and I numbly nod.

Jimmy now seems as if he's about to burst. "Well, we didn't put out garbage cans—I mean, like, ever. The cans stayed in the garage unused. Empty. Dad threw nothing out, so we never had any garbage. To put out, at least."

I consider this curiously stated fact. To the casual observer, we were in an average home: cluttered, sure, but not dirty and not that of a classic hoarder. All I can say in response is: "How is that possible?"

"It wasn't!" Jimmy attempts to explain. "It was impossible. Impossible to live like that. Impossible to keep that secret from relatives, from school, from the neighbors."

"Ugh, the neighbors," Tom agrees with a sigh. "I think they were the worst."

Our confused faces must have said more than any reply ever could.

Jimmy continues. "Think about it: This is Chicago. Row after row of nearly identical houses and driveways and nearly identical lives. Neighbors watch and gossip about each other, every fucking little thing. Who got a new car, a driveway repaved, a new roof or fence, a new baby, a new dog. These people have nothing else to talk about except one another. And if something isn't right or seems out of place, it's a big topic of interest."

"So," I say hesitatingly, "you never put out your garbage cans? Like that was a thing?"

"A huge thing!" Jimmy clarifies. "I mean, we're what? Twelve, thirteen years old. Neighbors, friends, and, shit, schoolmates actually called us 'the garbage can kids' cuz our dad never put trash cans out on Wednesday night— or any night, for that matter."

Tom adds, "People said we were dirty. I mean, we had to be, right? Because where did all our garbage go if it's not in the cans in the alley?"

Jimmy tries to shake off the memory. "We were teased about it constantly. Tormented, really. And from nearly everyone." He chokes up. "And the shame was—well, fuck, still is—the hardest part."

The garage grew warm. It seems as if we now had all gone too uncomfortably far into the story not to finally finish it.

"So . . . where did it go?" I ask sheepishly. "The trash, I mean."

Tom stoically prompted, "Tell them, Jimmy. Tell them."

Jimmy sits on stool beside a workbench and begins. "We'd take it to school with us. Or get rid of it on our way to school. Like, every day. On the street, the park, wherever we could find a garbage can. We'd sneak it out of the house in our backpacks, fold up the cardboard, put coffee grounds, leftovers, anything wet or smelly in a plastic bag and toss it wherever we could. It's the only time Dad would get really mad with us—if he caught us. He had to know what we were doing. Of course, it was hard to hide what we were doing—frickin' impossible, really—but we still did it. And if we didn't get the garbage out of the house fast, it'd stink up the place, especially the old food. For years, it was the only way to keep the house clean."

Tom moved closer to Jimmy and put his arm around him. "And to keep the secret. To keep Dad safe from what others might think of him . . . of us."

Jimmy starts to cry.

"And to keep us from being taken away," Tom continues. "Taken away from an otherwise really great dad."

Something unseen, unheard, but ever so critical . . . breaks. The brothers hug a long and long-overdue hug. Tears are wiped away from eight eyes.

Only then do Jeff and I begin to pack up the van with hundreds of old toys and dozens of new memories. We hug the brothers goodbye.

As we drove away, a thought caught my mind: Could a more wonderfully cathartic afternoon ever have been imagined from a random game of Clue?

CHAPTER 3

BEAT THE POET

Like many teens, I didn't know what I wanted to do with my life. I was a good student, but math, science, and every foreign language confounded me. I enjoyed writing yet had no confidence I could turn such interest into a single dollar, let alone a career. I seemed incapable of learning an instrument; my musical interests included only the collecting of Broadway show tunes, an off-key note, if not ominous warning of my variant sexuality.

The bullying in high school had only hardened me on the outside and turned me into a skittish jangle of nerves on the inside. I constructed a defensive wall around myself to protect my gelatinously sensitive interior. In short, I had the confidence of a soft-boiled egg. Messy.

My sister, Bonita, was nine years my senior, and I adored every beautiful bit of her. Born in 1950 with a neuro-blastoma tumor on one of her kidneys, she was treated with deep X-ray therapy that would ultimately leave her sterile. Her life was a constant medical struggle, and her cancer returned time and again throughout her brief life. Still, she persevered, if not thrived. Nothing came easy for her—health, school, friends, boyfriends—but she powered through it all without complaint. She endured decades of chemotherapy and troubles only the biblical Job would understand. She was, and still is, my hero.

After high school and a brief stint as a hairdresser, my sister decided to become a teacher. She so loved children, and while unable to have any of her own, the choice to teach the children of others fulfilled a personal goal. She took assorted classes at various colleges and then steeled herself to become a special education teacher through the offerings of Northeastern Illinois University (NIU) in Chicago. It would prove to be a turning point in both our lives.

Again, as a graduating teen, I was lost. When my parents met my high school's guidance counselor, they were presented with an application for Northwestern University in Evanston and the staggeringly commen-surate estimate of what such an education would cost.

"He's smart!" said the counselor. "He has very good grades, and his writing is, um, interesting. Rather creative. Yes, I think he's an excellent candidate for Northwestern."

My mother looked at the tuition estimate. "Is that for a year?" she bristled. "You must be kidding me. Our *house* didn't cost that much!"

"Perhaps he could get a scholarship in a year or two," he offered.

"Yeah," my dad mumbled slowly. "Um, no."

I'm certain lives are turned on more dramatic narratives than this, but that was that: any possibility of my ever attending Northwestern University or being part of their famous *Mee-Ow Show*, a musical comedy review put on by the students, stopped right there. On the upside, my parents said I could get a cat.

Short story long, I followed my sister's path . . . to NIU, where I, too, would almost/sorta/kinda become a teacher. I double majored in English and secondary education with a minor in theatre—or more accurately, drama—most of it occurring in my parents' kitchen in the form of hysterical tantrums.

You see, I was very unhappy, especially with myself. I was short, cripplingly shy as previously detailed, and to anyone fully conscious, overtly gay. I was effeminate, had a speech impediment, and spent the proceeds from my first part-time job on a secondhand mink coat. And yes, a ladies' mink coat because I couldn't find a man's coat in my size: X-tra gay, chromosome small.

I came out to my parents in my early teens, but they simply weren't having it. "No, you're not!" was about as close as I ever got to my parents' acceptance. My mother seemed to believe that repeating a phrase over and over would effect a change. I would remind her that screaming, "On the newspaper!" when housebreaking our rotating collection of poodles had never been effective. They certainly never became readers.

Something had to change, and I knew it wasn't going to be me or our newspaper subscription.

Once in college, I slowly started to bloom. I met students of other nationalities, races, and religions. When I met my first lesbian—one never forgets their first lesbian—I thought I would explode. Not that we had much in common. "No dick for me!" she'd laugh. But I'd found someone who understood my sad, lonely self. We bonded over our virginity and lack of BFs/GFs. It was an odd yet strangely satisfying friendship.

I realized that as wonderful as my parents had been—truly giving me everything I had ever needed or wanted—it still wasn't enough. I was miserable, and I had to get out of their house. I had to find a way to break away, to be self-sufficient personally and financially, to grow up and move out. But how to accomplish this?

I now understood why my parents hadn't sent me to Northwestern—the debt would have been overwhelming— but there was more to this than met the all-seeing eye on the dollar bill of cost. In paying my tuition, my parents controlled my decisions and limited my autonomy. My mother had one hard, nonnegotiable house rule: No son of hers could move out before marriage. And she meant to a woman. And that wasn't about to happen—like, ever. Sam Houston, we have a problem.

Still, there was a silver lining to the wreckage of my missed Northwestern education: a scholarship. No, not from the direction northwest, but from the northeast. If I could score a scholarship from Northeastern Illinois University, I could plot the exit from my parent's home. Brideless, yes, but in search of seven brothers, one of whom, odds were, had to be gay.

Within a few short days of NIU scholarship sleuthing, I had unearthed three potential offerings: (1) a fiction writing scholarship, (2) a playwriting scholarship, and (3) a poetry scholarship. The first two were daunting and required the writing of a novel and a play, respectively. The poetry scholarship demanded the writing of a dozen or so poems, which I quickly dismissed as silly.

For the next six months, I threw myself into the anguished but fashionable shoes of F. Scott Fitzgerald and Edward Albee, my two heroes at the time. I read some Sylvia Plath but found her poems, not to mention her fate, too depressing to stalk, literarily speaking.

In the category of "Novels That Blow for $100" I submitted *Insanityland,* a novel loosely inspired by

Kerouac's *On the Road* by way of an off-ramp exit toward *The Wizard of Oz*. To this day, the manuscript is buried in a box somewhere, no doubt frightening a judgmental spider.

In the category of "Failed Plays Almost Produced," I submitted *Da Buck,* a violent black comedy involving parents and their two children who have a contest to see who can make the most money by killing their neighbors one by one. No, it wasn't a musical, sadly. However, this opus had multiple readings at NIU's theatre wing, shockingly, until the department chair got wind of it (see: more blowing).

Now for the poetry scholarship: honestly, I scarcely tried. I dashed off verses by the baker's dozen and barely remembered sealing the envelope of submission. I knew I was going to be the next Kurt Vonnegut or Christopher Durang. Fuck Sylvia Plath's Nazi lampshades (see: Lady Lazarus). I was on the path to better lighting and microwave cooking.

I'm sure you know where this is going by now. I was awarded a four-year poetry scholarship, one of only two offered by the university, proving that life is often a kick in the Balzac. Gwendolyn Brooks, the poet laureate of Illinois at the time, no less, had personally chosen the winners. And she had recently succeeded Carl Sandburg, the state's previous poet laureate. *Maybe I wasn't half bad.*

Prior to the scholarship, I took a few poetry classes and was dismissive of them at best. I remember that they were filled with some of the strangest people I had ever met, then or now. For instance, the woman who drove two hours every day to attend the poetry workshop, only to read aloud her poems of grisly automobile accidents witnessed during her commute. Seriously. "The mangled crush of chrome upon flesh; the twisted tollbooth change never given; carnage equally unforgiving." Et cetera.

Commenting on those opuses was always the same: *I abstain from any carpooling with her, thanks.*

Another student, actually a rather brilliant one, would recite the poems he had written while on whatever opiate of the day he had scored in the university parking lot. His poems were non sequiturs of gibberish, metaphors mixed in morphine-lite, but he was rather handsome with a long, luxurious mane of brown hair and an equally follicle-perfect beard. So we all agreed—straight or gay—he was a wonderfully dreamy, if not suitably fuckable, poet.

But I digress from this mess. In fact, I was somewhat ashamed that the thing I had put the least amount of effort into—these poems I spit into existence simply to check a scholarship box—had become my personal cornerstone. I was good friends with the other poetry winner, a lovely young lady who wrote very pretty verses, often about housekeeping. Or at least that's what I recall.

The two of us would soon find ourselves joined at the lyrical hip as we embraced our mutual good fortune.

As financially freeing as these scholarships were, they came with a catch: whenever the English department deemed our mini poetry slams necessary, we both had to read, or more accurately, perform. I could return to my trained-poodle metaphor of paragraphs past, but I shall refrain. I was damn lucky to have anyone think I could provide a lick of entertainment that didn't require swallowing my pride or anything else for that matter.

Still, no performance would be as important as our first public appearance before a tony assembly of professors, department chairs, countless wives, and (gulp) the university president and his delicate spouse. Held in the university's auditorium, the formal affair was attended by the well-dressed and equally well-heeled staff and those similarly noteworthy. It was a heady afternoon of congratulatory speeches, glad-handing, and backslapping, with the presentation of two new poetic discoveries and their respective readings as the main event.

Whatever could go right . . . went over their heads!

Of course, Gwendolyn Brooks presided over these honors. A handsome Black woman, she wore a beautifully tailored suit with a white ruffled collar. She looked exquisitely Elizabethan, while I, in my jeans and black T-shirt, undoubtedly looked untailored.

First up to read was my comrade in poetry scholarship. Gwendolyn said a few charming words of introduction that I no longer remember. I was panicking in my gym shoes, having never performed before a group so, so . . . smartly put together. My fellow scholarship winner read a few of her home economics-themed poems; today, I can only remember a single line from one of them: "Tomorrow, I shall leave le dishes in le sink . . ."

It was as French as fries, but she received a pleasantly polite round of applause from the crowd.

Again with the housework, I think. I feared for her attempt to rhyme any word with "Electrolux" without the obvious off-color match.

Gwendolyn returned to the stage and introduced me with these words: "I believe this next young man has the strength of words to make something great over the long haul of life." Um. Wow. What does that mean? In retrospect, she was damn prophetic, but in the moment, I was dumbfounded.

In the center of the stage, I hesitated and began. "This poem is called . . . 'LSD Consumes 47 Times Its Weight in Excess Reality.'" And I went on with:

Slalom

Slipping swiftly down a mountain

Dodging Buicks, avoiding Volvos

Skiing down a corkscrew noodle

My feet sliced red in the hot tomato goo

Wet dreams of prince macaroni

And our Wednesday afternoon.

But I know

We've got to stop

Skiing each other on the sly

On the slopes of your bed

The mountains of your body.

To me, living rent free in your valley

Is more costly than city slumming.

I looked into the crowd and saw the tortured face of the university president's wife; her hand on her mouth as if attempting to hold in an uncontrollable scream. Similar faces reflected back, but then, slowly, soft clapping began. Initiated by Gwendolyn, she moved toward me, beaming.

The clapping grew a tad louder as she leaned into my ear and whispered, "See! You make people listen. Read another one."

I was dizzy with excitement, and yes, empowerment. My shyness disappeared, and I spoke with a sharpening precision, fearlessly focusing my words on the crowd. My life would never again be withdrawn. Finally, I was happy to be who I was.

I cleared my throat and announced: "My next poem is called . . . 'Perversion Is for Lovers.'"

You / have this thing / about dwarves / hunky gnomes / little men in chicken suits / and women extra crispy / to the lick of foreign tongues

And I do not question your social life.

You / spend your days / giggling in your darkened room / the curdled sound of circus people / crawling through the woodwork / flushing through the plumbing

And I do not question your social life.

You / paint the walls / with whip cream / leather boots slicing through the froth / as squeals elicit moans / and pleading wails into low, luscious laughter

And I do not question your social life.

You / have spent a lifetime / in ecstasy / in teeth marked little men / in feisty little women / in perversions far beyond mere degradation

And I do not question your social life.

Because . . . I am you.

In the original margins of the poem's page, Gwendolyn Brooks had written: "This is the winner of the Northeastern Illinois Poetry Scholarship, 1980."

In the parlance of that well-worn comedy club compliment, I killed.

I would later learn that Ms. Brooks's most famous poem, "We Real Cool," was banned from being read in the Mississippi and West Virginia classrooms of the 1970s. Along with authors such as Allen Ginsberg, D. H. Lawrence, and Walt Whitman, Gwendolyn Brooks joined a banned brotherhood that, in the end, made them even more respected. And a lot more famous.

Perhaps she saw that same rebellion of language in me. Yes, I made people listen. I learned very quickly that without a first foothold of shocked attention, a writer's successful journey is nearly impossible.

My sister—and, most assuredly, Gwendolyn Brooks—changed my life. I didn't become a schoolteacher; I became a poet—a lyricist, actually. I went on to cocreate, along with musical wunderkind David Brian Bell, one of the first house music labels in the country (Persona Records) and became an unwitting pioneer in a now globally recognized genre.

My tone poem "Civil Defense" has remained in print—on vinyl, actually—and a dance floor staple for over thirty-five years. It's been bootlegged around the world, and original copies—which I no longer own— sell for big bucks.

Now if that's not "the long haul of life," I don't know what is.

Today, I am signed to Les Disques De La Mort, a French music label, the irony not lost on those unwashed dishes in le sink.

FOUR SISTERS AND A FUNERAL

It begins with a phone call.

"Hello? Yes, we buy furniture. Oh, I'm very sorry for your loss. Yes, we know the building. Yes. It's very tall—high-rises often are. Oh, how awful. Terrible. Yes, very sad. And she was your sister? You're in town only for a brief time? Time constraints. Yes, we understand. Liquidating the estate quickly, yes. What's the address, unit number? Yes, a high floor—you mentioned. You've already secured an elevator for the day—excellent. Yes, we receive many calls a day just like this. Yes, always very sad."

A few hours later, my partner, Jeff, and I arrive at the estate. Fortunately, we are able to catch our furniture movers, Tee Jay and his crew. They had planned to go fishing on Lake Michigan—their party plans starting early—but now we've intervened with a very different catch of the day.

We enter a nondescript apartment from the 1970s, a high-floor, two-bedroom unit smartly furnished in an efficient mid-century modern fashion; nothing particularly design worthy but still many simple, practical vintage pieces.

Three elderly women greet us at the door; one sobs softly into her handkerchief. "It's our sister Ida," says the smallest of the three. "She passed suddenly, and we're selling the contents of the apartment immediately. Everything is for sale."

The middle sister interjects nervously. "Well, not *everything's* for sale; you know what I mean. Some things, well, one thing, I mean . . . isn't for sale."

The third sister muffles out a tearful "No!" and points to a sofa in the living room.

The smallest sister continues: "Sirs, if you please, not the sofa bed." She moves closer to us, away from her other sisters, and drops her voice to a whisper. "If at all possible, please don't even mention the sofa bed. Everything else is for sale, of course. Just make us fair offers; that's all we ask. We do have other buyers coming shortly." She returns to stand beside her sisters, shouting, "Birdy, isn't someone else coming later?" Louder still: "With *cash?*"

A distracted Birdy either mishears or ignores her sister's questions. No one else responds, and I duck back into the outer hallway as my partner surveys the furniture for potential sale.

Our movers remain near the freight-elevator doors at the ready. "Okay, guys, here's the deal," I begin. "I'll point out the pieces we're buying. Only take the items that I show you. Now, there's an old brown sofa bed in the living room. Do *not* take that piece. Also, do not even ask about it. They're all elderly ladies who are very sensitive about what just happened. So zip it, okay?"

A mixed grumbling of English and Spanish seems to accept the situation. I return to the apartment, check-book in hand.

By this point, Jeff has purchased a dining room table and six chairs, a sideboard, a pair of nightstands, and an ottoman. All '60s–'70s pieces, all practical, well-made, useable items. The sisters appear to be motivated sellers, and it's a fast, easy negotiation for a buy-it-all final price. I quickly write the check.

As the movers lumber into the room, Jeff and I are pointing out: "This table, that China hutch, those dining chairs," and it's all leaving the apartment like clockwork—except we're not buying the wall clock. It's broken. After twenty-five busy minutes of multiple trips on the freight elevator, every piece is carried to the building's loading dock and into a giant moving truck.

We return to the apartment to give our final condolences and a fast goodbye.

"It was all so sudden!" begins the smallest sister. "We were all so very close, even though we live in different parts of the country. But it did make it easier to meet here in the middle . . . in Chicago. Just so sad it had to be for poor Ida's funeral."

The quietest of the sisters waves a faltering handkerchief, and Birdy holds her up with exhaustive effort. "Yesterday," the softest sister sighs. "She died right here in the apartment." She points a crooked finger at the old brown sofa bed. "There. She died right there barely twelve hours ago . . ."

Birdy, timing clearly not her forte, now feels compelled to chime in to the sad tale. "When they took her body away, the cushions stayed warm for hours, but I think they can be dry-cleaned."

On that uncomfortable note, the wailing starts up again, and the frailest of the three is led off to sit on the one chair we didn't buy. FYI: bad split on the armrest.

Slowly, we attempt our exit, expressing our further condolences and thanking each sister with a careful hug so as not to break their China-doll fragility, all the while contemplating the meter fees ticking up on the multiple vehicles we have (barely legally) parked downstairs.

Stepping backward out of the unit, we suddenly knock into our lead mover, Tee Jay, who has inexplicably decided to return to the apartment. "Did we forget something?" I ask, hinting to him that we certainly hadn't. But Tee Jay doesn't take the hint.

"Oh, no," he says, bumbling back into the unit with his usual ignorance-is-bliss enthusiasm, making a torpedo-like jaunt into the living room with a single upholstered target in mind. "So how come we're not taking the sofa bed with us?" he quizzes. "Is something wrong with it?"

Jeff and I simultaneously shout out, "They're keeping it!"

But Tee Jay is oblivious, a trait he's long crafted into a thickheaded science.

Now Birdy joins her louder sibling, and the three begin to wail like dying smoke detectors.

In the middle of all this, we chime, "We're sorry, so sorry," and other excuses, but the words cannot be taken back. Clearly both Elvis—and a dead sister—have left the building. This show is seriously over.

What could possibly make this any more embarrassing? Wait for it. Wait for it.

Yes, Tee Jay begins to upend the sofa bed, holding it squarely above his head like he's the would-be strongman of the vintage circus, and examines the bed's bottom. "Doesn't seem to be anything wrong with it."

He turns to us. "Isn't this old enough, guys? You could sell this thing for sure . . ."

I thought I heard one of the three sisters scream out a high-pitched "Oh my god!" Then again, it was probably me.

Birdy quickly shuffles over to Tee Jay and starts slow-motion slapping him with a wrinkled hand, shouting, "She died on that bed—died right where you're standing!"

Split-second quick, Tee Jay suddenly pushes himself away from the sofa bed as it falls from his hands like a burnt trout on a hot plate. Go fish!

The crying. The shouting. The sound of the sofa bed hitting the floor, echoing half a dozen floors below. It reminds me of that old Three Stooges short *There's Been a Murder*. The stooges are suspects. Someone points out to Curly that he's standing on the exact spot where the dead man once stood. Curly shouts a "Woo-woo-woo" and immediately levitates right out of his own shoes. Funny stuff.

Except this wasn't funny but, instead, horribly embarrassing.

Tee Jay wipes his gloves on himself as if he's trying to clean away the memory of the all-too-recent death. Yet he still keeps on blathering: "Hey, I'm sorry. I didn't know your sister croaked right there. Jeez, that's too bad. Just last night, was it? I was watching the game;

Cubs lost again, but she probably missed it, right? A shame, really. But hey, you gals sure got rid of her stuff in a hurry!"

A glacially slow moment passes, then Tee Jay asks, "So how old was she?"

Birdy chirps: "Seventy-nine!"

"Oh, she was up there then; her time to go, no doubt . . ."

"She was the youngest!" replies an octogenarian chorus.

Now I bodily push Tee Jay out the front door while Jeff pushes me in the same direction. Somehow, the three of us are momentarily lodged within the door frame in our race to exit the apartment. We all fall into the hallway and tumble toward the freight elevator, resale tails between our legs.

Tee Jay turns back to the women with his final comments. "Oh, and my sincerest condolences," he says with a half-hearted bow. "Um, nice apartment!"

With all of us—and the last of the furnishings—packed solidly into the elevator, we begin our slow descent to the loading dock. I turn to Tee Jay. "You had to say something after I specifically told you *not* to mention the sofa bed! Goddamn it, what is wrong with you?"

"Relax, no big whoop!" He sighs, obliviously scratching his butt against the corner of a teak sideboard. "It's just dead people's things."

Postscript:

1. We have since parted ways with Tee Jay; in fact, sadly, Tee Jay has parted ways with the world itself. On a brighter note, we now have an incredible new mover who practically has a fan club. Buy a piece of furniture from us and you, too, can join the club.

2. For the record, this story is not how my first book's title was derived. "Dead people's things" is a phrase antiques dealers have used for decades, if not centuries; it's an industry parlance that captures, perhaps somewhat crudely, the essence of those objects that provide us "a living." So Tee Jay was not inaccurate in his comment. Inappropriate and badly timed, yes, but true. Still, on completion of my previous book, I decided the final title required something actionable. Perhaps a subtle verb could provide the right tone? The word "selling" seemed best in evoking the commerce of it all. The rest, as I am prone to say, is my immediate history.

CHAPTER 5

SORROWS OF THE MAD HATTER

At precisely 11:20 a.m., a gleaming executive transport vehicle pulls up to O'Hare Airport's American Airlines terminal gate 227 and parks alongside the busy check-in counter.

The vehicle's driver, Robert, takes these last few minutes to prepare, fastidiously touching up his electric cart with a ready cloth. A decades-long employee of the airline, he possesses that crucial time-efficient trait placing him in the company's top tier of celebrity transportation managers.

Whether shuttling presidents, kings, popes, or pop stars, his level of professionalism is always the same: bring that notable individual to their destination with discretion and, above all else, safety.

Now he turns his attention to the job at hand, adjusting his tie, running a quick comb through his thinning hair, but most important, double-checking his celebrity manifest. Only then can he stand confidently and attentively at the ready for the disembarking first-class passengers.

Glancing away from the line of travelers for barely a moment, he almost misses the sight of a razor-slight figure in a paisley-print miniskirt. How could anyone mistake those bony legs for anyone other than today's celebrity? Still, it would have been hard not to notice that riotous, rooster-pitched laughter from one of the most famous comedians on the planet.

"Ms. Diller," he half shouts across the terminal's noisy din.

Immediately, she recognizes him, saying, "Robert, my good man. How the hell are you?"

By now, other passengers in the terminal recognize—or more likely hear—the outrageously dressed figure in question. Robert reaches for her single leopard-print carry-on bag and dutifully assists the iconic Phyllis Diller into his readied transport vehicle. "How was your flight, Ms. Diller?" queries Robert, plopping his ample frame behind the steering wheel.

"Ha!" she exclaims at an earsplitting decibel. "I think the pilot wanted me to join the mile high club, but I told him my body was a no-fly zone!"

Robert holds in a laugh, discretionary composure being a paramount to his company position. "That's very, very funny!" he replies while maneuvering his vehicle through the busy crisscrossing throngs of airport passengers.

"Funny?" Diller deadpans, leaning forward in her seat and closer to Robert's ear. "Come on, that was hysterical. I'm breaking in new material. I used all my old material to buy this dress, if you can call it a dress. It's Frederick's of Hollywood Lawn. I'm going to be cremated in it if my body doesn't spontaneously combust first!"

Robert, in considerable abdominal pain from containing his laughter, repeats the words, *Focus, focus,* in his head. The terminal's frantic crowd now slows his vehicle as more people do a double take on seeing the flamboyantly recognizable Phyllis Diller.

Shouts begin to ring out from the stirring crowd, cameras appearing in every simultaneous direction. "Ms. Diller, Ms. Diller! It's Phyllis Diller. Can we get a photo? An autograph? Look at the hat she's wearing—outrageous!"

Robert distracts himself from the passenger's tumult as he slows his vehicle, asking: "Are you playing the Blue Max at the Hyatt Regency again, Ms. Diller?"

"Two weeks!" she shouts back, waving at her fans. Leaning forward again, she whispers, "But don't stop for autographs. I need to get to the hotel before these pantyhose are repossessed—I bought them at an exorcist's estate sale."

Suddenly spotting an aisle shortcut, Robert veers his transport vehicle into a less populated terminal byway and hits the electric acceleration pedal.

Phyllis Diller grabs the huge, crazy hat sitting precariously atop her head. "Robert," she shouts into the sudden breeze against her face, "you're like my favorite candy on the Titanic." She screams, "A lifesaver!"

He slows his speed as the vehicle passes through a special oversized doorway and parks beside an awaiting limousine. Another celebrity safely transported.

"Any shopping trips planned while you're in Chicago?" Robert asks, holding her hand as he assists her out of the vehicle and returns her bag.

With the door of the limousine now held open by its chauffer, Phyllis Diller turns, takes off her elaborate, oversized headdress, and ferociously shakes it in Robert's direction. "Of course, my dear," she booms with her trademarked guffaw. "I need another half dozen of these babies. Momma just loves her hats!"

* * *

Raymond Hudd, aka the Mad Hatter of the Midwest, stands meekly before me at the sales counter of my store, Wrigleyville Antiques in Chicago. It is 1992. I am thirty-three years old, and he is sixty-eight.

Spread across the counter are film canisters, small film-developing tanks, camera lenses, tiny sterling silver camera charms, and assorted toy plastic cameras, almost everything diminutive in scale. The debate at the moment is whether these items can be disassembled and reassembled in such a way as to preserve their "look" as actual camera parts and pieces and not—as Mr. Hudd presently refers to them—as "Junk!"

"I don't know," he sighs with indecision. "I just don't know."

"Let me guess," I offer with a jibe. "You're designing a hat dedicated to Abraham Zapruder? Assassination chic!"

He bursts into giggles, his eyes sparking with the joke. "Oh, you are so, so bad." And then: "But I love that idea . . . Imagine a little Jackie Kennedy doll and her little pill-box hat. Oh my god, you are such a naughty boy."

Raymond Hudd is famous for many things: his "headline" or "news-in-review" hats are based on many stirring moments of the day, most notably the fall of the Berlin Wall, Oliver North's Iran–Contra scandal, the Tylenol poisoning murders, his "death from smoking" chapeau with its coffin-nail-styled cigarettes, etc. Once he even used a surgically removed gallstone as an inspiration for a hat. But he is most famously known for his artfully whimsical millinery work for such stars as Joan Crawford, Phyllis Diller, Barbara Eden, Ann

Landers, and countless others. Or as he often refers to them, "My ladies."

Perhaps most peculiar, he is equally famous for founding the Space Age Club, an organization of alien abductees, in 1959. Naturally, there is an iconic Sputnik hat and assorted UFO-themed headdresses in his ever-widening design collection. However, that's another story and galaxy we won't soon be visiting.

Today, we're deep into another earthbound problem entirely: you see, it is one of the great simple joys of my life as an antiques dealer to assist artists like Raymond Hudd in sourcing unique materials for their work. To the layman, this would appear a simple task. Often, it is not. In Mr. Hudd's fashionable world, innumerable little details need to be addressed. And I do mean *little*.

Consider his camera hat of the moment: Raymond Hudd has conceived the hat's concept, structural design, physical shape, all-so-important fabric choice, fabrication, and vital purpose all in his whirring, idea-filled head.

I, of course, have not a clue. My job—and I am blessed to even call it that—is to locate objects that complement the concept of this project yet remain both diminutive in scale and nearly weightless. Remember, it's a hat. It is art, first and foremost, but it also must be comfortable, fashion-forward, and dare I say futuristic. It needs to be, well, a *chapeau* great enough to be called a Raymond Hudd hat.

The assembly of all these seemingly disparate elements takes time. I am certainly not the only person assisting this famous haberdasher at his milliner's craft, but I take his requests as if he is client number one for innumerable reasons.

I recall one particular project in which he wanted to create a hat completely covered in miniature Eiffel Towers. Easy, right? Well, no, because many of the vintage souvenir Eiffel Towers produced were not only known for their large scale—who wants a small Eiffel Tower?—but were almost always made of metal or, worse yet, an ugly and impractically heavy resin.

I scour the Midwest for over year in search of tiny plastic Eiffel Towers—basically the cheapest ones, as I would soon discover, and the scarcest. Again, Mr. Hudd wants vintage, not new. So I will shop hundreds of thrift and antiques store, picking up one little plastic Eiffel Tower at a time. When I have some thirty Eiffel Towers in *mon petit les mains,* I contact the artistic Mr. Hudd, who is at my door within the hour.

If only you could have seen his face: souvenir ecstasy. I was so happy with his response that I didn't even charge him. What a thrill it was to simply be a part of something so magical. Today, I'm fairly certain this carefully crafted Eiffel Tower hat is in a museum somewhere or in a treasured collection eventually bound for same.

Raymond Hudd shops my store almost monthly. We have, to be cautiously honest, an almost affectionate relationship *sans* the romance; a mutually curious though unfulfilled puppy dog crush on one another that may sound offbeat to most. He sometimes flirts with me and I with him in an innocence found only in an earlier century or, perhaps, in a gay remake of *Harold and Maude*, or better still, Harold and Maudlin.

If I were older or he were younger, I'd tell myself, but neither was true and that was the end of it. What is the mutual attraction? We both love "the stuff" and leave it at that. Still, I am charmed that he is so open with me about his life, his art, and most proudly, his stores dubbed Raymond Hudd Registered Originals, first located on Chicago's tony Oak Street then later in fashionable Lincoln Park. These locations, in their day, were both as famous as he.

Mr. Hudd encourages me to hang framed photographs of the many celebrities who pass through my store: Anthony Quinn, John Candy, Rita Wilson, Bob Balaban, Beck, Oliver Stone, etc. "Customers just love seeing celebrity photos!" he'd exclaim. "It makes them feel that they're part of something bigger, something special." And he is right.

Perhaps because we have this special friendship, bonding over "the stuff" and our chats about life and love, I believe Raymond Hudd feels comfortable enough to tell me an incredible, if not shocking, story.

* * *

Sadly, it begins with the sudden death of Raymond's brother, throwing Mr. Hudd's world into chaos that few could traverse without stumbling. He has the necessary funeral plans to arrange, family and friends to contact, and a thousand details to handle, all the while closing up his one-man-band of a milliner's shop. He has obligations there as well: ordered hats to make and ship and promises to keep, both personal and professional. It is all too much, too fast, too soon.

A few short days after his brother's burial, Raymond returns to his store, nervously unlocking the door, his mind a grieving blank, yet he tries to focus on putting his life—and most important, his business—back on track.

Raymond, now in his seventies, is seated on the floor of his shop behind a long display counter that runs parallel to his store's front door. He's putting out a few new hats and fluffing up some older stock when his door suddenly opens to reveal six legs, those of a skirted woman flanked by two men in black slacks. Imagine this:

he's looking from floor level, mind you, through his own display cases at the legs of three strangers.

"I'll be up in a minute," he says, attempting to finish the display work he's started. However, the three figures move closer to the counter, and he can hear the woman pulling hats off the countertop mannequin's heads willy-nilly, as he would later relate. Big mistake.

To be clear, Raymond Hudd, artist, milliner, and showman, always permits his ladies to try on his hats. Always. But there is also a method to the madness of this hatter—a procedure, as it were. Raymond offers suggestions when presenting a hat to a client, hands her the hat, and shows how it should be held when not worn; finally, he proffers ideas on how it should be placed on one's head and styled. He is, to be clear, the Mad Hatter of the Midwest, for goodness' sake, and has been such an expert for some fifty years. The man knows what he's doing.

Raymond is a bit winded and struggles to stand upright, still distraught over the recent death of his brother. He pulls himself up from floor and shouts, "Please! Please, do not touch the hats!"

It is only when he is 100 percent vertical that he realizes he is standing before an internationally famous talk show host, her driver, and a bodyguard. He is speechless. She is not.

"Well," she disappointedly sighs, turning on her designer shoes. "I thought we were in the shop of hatmaker Mr. Raymond Hudd. Our mistake."

And just like that, *poof,* she's gone. In less than a minute, it was all over. It didn't matter that he hadn't heard the little *tinkle-tinkle* of the bell he had affixed to the top of his shop's door, because now, with the great lady's exit, the last *tinkle* faded out lifeless like a dying echo of an opportunity lost.

In this retelling, Raymond is in near tears. You see, Raymond Hudd was, is, and will always be the number-one fan of this celebrated woman, considering her a near goddess. She personifies what he so admires: women who came from humble, if not desperate, beginnings and took on the world in conquering success; his favorite movie stars all mimic the rags-to-riches stories, these Horatio Alger tales in heels. Raymond's own life echoes such a life path of struggle and success.

Born Raymond Huddlestun in 1925 on a truck farm in Custer, Michigan, his fertile imagination would run rampant in their small home while his brothers worked the fertile fields. His first hat design was for their two barnyard mules, Fanny and Jack, a pair of mud-and-leaves hats that took as long to perfect as it did to train the mules to wear. By 1948, he was attending the School of the Art Institute of Chicago and two years later opened his first shop, attending to the needs of Chicago's high society set. His meteoric rise in the local fashion scene was as short as his newly shortened name: Hudd.

When I ask why he never moved to New York City to take a swing at further fame, he tells me, "I'd rather be a big fish in a smaller pond."

But now, that greater fame and acclaim, one he might never even intended to pursue, will never be realized. Tragically, nay, accidentally, one of the greatest success stories in the world of entertainment has not only sought him out, but he'd inadvertently insulted her, seemingly to walk out his life forever.

In the days that follow, Raymond Hudd calls her famous studio, leaving heartfelt messages of apology and stuttering explanations to a tone-deaf switchboard. He sends cards. He sends flowers. And in his most sincere act of confessed remorse, he designs a few hats in exclusive tribute to the woman and forwards them along in magnificently styled hatboxes. But all are returned: cards unread; flowers dead; hat boxes unopened; the dazzling Raymond Hudd hats unworn.

Through tears, perhaps cathartic, each retelling of the story brings no closure to the event, the misstep, a social faux pas. The incident replays over in his mind with many *what-ifs* along the way. With seemingly unnecessary guilt, he admonishes his own sharp tongue and the unfortunate circumstance of a singularly special moment missed:

- Had my brother not passed the previous week
- Had I been standing upright behind the counter when the trio arrived rather than seated on the floor
- Had I not said the harsh words

It was, without question, an accident. Something unforeseen had happened, and there was no way it could be unraveled or undone. Like a fragile bow on a most beautiful hat, this ribbon pulled could never again be tied.

During his lifetime, Raymond Hudd, who passed in 2011, would go on to design some fifty thousand original hats, using every conceivable and inconceivable material. He was brilliant. He was eccentric. He was a genius. But he certainly was never "mad," unless defined as creatively so.

Phyllis Diller would amass some five hundred Raymond Hudd original creations, a few finding their way to the auction of her own fabulous estate.

Before his salon closed in the late 1990s, countless other famous ladies would arrive time and again to be dazzled at the altar of the magic milliner, Mr. Raymond Hudd, the Mad Hatter of the Midwest.

A life well-lived went on. Museums held Raymond Hudd retrospectives. His work has been sold and resold via eBay, Etsy, and the RealReal, finding its way into the closets and hearts of adoring fans and fashionistas by the tens of thousands.

So, no—ironically and perhaps a bit poetically—this story doesn't feature a "headline" hat.

It will, however, be news to most. And that is most perfectly fitting.

CHAPTER 6

BEATEN
BY THE
BEAUTIFUL

In high school, I was voted "Most likely to be disliked."

There was never a need for an actual election, as it was more of a general consensus among most of the student body and, apparently, some of the staff. I learned, quite quickly, that if one was going to be disliked, there was no sense in going halfway. Middle school taught me that. Heck, kindergarten had practically been foreplay.

Now, some may consider this a bad thing—being disliked, I mean—but I believe it's always better to know where you stand, especially when submerged. Being "out" in high school was bound to be the cause of trouble for most anyone. Honestly, I thought if Oscar Wilde could handle it in the 1870s, I could surely pull this off in the 1970s. I mean, the collars were just as wide and the pants even wider. And like it says in both the Bible and on the letterhead of the RNC, what's a millennium between sodomites?

There was little I could do about my situation at the time. I was barely five feet tall, weighed less than one hundred pounds, had acne, was rather effeminate, and could do a mean Paul Lynde imitation. Further, as there were no other Danish-Czechoslovakian kids in the school, or on the United States continent, I had free roam of my own ruination.

Decades later, my alcohol-infused self would realize that when life gives you lemons, make limoncello. But at fourteen, I had yet to arrive at this sour revelation, and my lemonlike life only squeezed out a bitter truth: I was a fruit. Of course, this was one of the kinder linguistic slurs of the day from a list of gay-laced references that could fill this page and many more.

My least favorite back-and-forth taunts would go something like: "Do you have pubic hair in your teeth?"

An answer of no returned the reply: "Well, would you like some?" Which, of course, is the gay-baiter's version of "Do you still beat your wife?"

If I answered yes, that would often scare the crap out of anyone who asked the original question. Hence, my well-earned fame in the pantheon of the disliked. Under such conditions, how could I not feel as if I were working in a gay adolescent's version of the Catskills? Whether you're heckled onstage or off in some distant corner of the lunchroom, the deflection in life is the same.

More than once, I told some dumb harassing joker that he should find new material, hire someone funny, preferably Jewish, as they were an infinitely less talented Christian Kringle. This response never stopped the abuse, but it gave me a true boost of self-confidence to see their puzzled faces grimacing back. I was thrilled with the oft-repeated review to their puberty-addled classmates: "That kid is weird!"

Defiantly, I would often wear tiny Sears Roebuck blazers and bow ties—rather pre-Pee-wee Herman by way of an abbreviated Quentin Crisp. So yes, it was mostly my fault. I was obsessed with Edward Everett Horton, Charles Nelson Reilly, and Truman Capote, especially when he argued with Gore Vidal on the *Dick Cavett Show*. In fact, for my freshman Halloween costume, I dressed as Gore Vidal, wearing a simple black suit: very elegant, very dandyesque.

Plus, I had a few pithy retorts for anyone questioning my costume choice: "Diana Vreeland said I'm tastier than white chocolate mousse at a Harlem speakeasy!" or "Get away from me before someone drops a house on your sister. But it sure won't be happening to you with *those* shoes!" and "I wouldn't talk to you if you were picking up Jackie Kennedy's dry cleaning after the assassination!" You get the idea.

Back then, I was beaten up by many people: mostly strangers, but an occasional friend or three—too many blurry faces in the crowd to recall. Still, somehow, I knew I was on to something.

My sophomore Halloween costume was Cousin Itt from *The Addams Family*—easy, given my sister's access to dozens of wigs and other beauty supplies to complete the look. My lack of height, intentionally garbled language of gibberish, and floor-length hair extensions made me the hit of the cafeteria. Let me tell you: nothing bounces better off four industrial-size cans of Aqua Net than day-old lime Jell-O.

My junior year Halloween costume was no less weird: I came dressed as dead Walt Disney—no easy feat, as he'd passed a decade earlier from lung cancer. The rumor was that Uncle Walt had been cryogenically frozen so he could return in the future to smoke yet another carton of cigarettes daily. Like the Andy Kaufman rumor mill many years later, both seemed like the kind of fellows who could pull off just such a stunt. So, whether it was a full body freezing or just one's head preserved in a large pickle jar, we kids just ate up the possibilities. Or at least I did. It's a small, weird world after all, especially if you can only afford the jar.

In keeping with the looming urban Disney myth, I wore a sharp black burial suit with long clear plastic Christmas icicles hanging from my hat. In retrospect, who gets buried wearing a hat? I mean, you can die with your boots on, but you always take off your hat. And icicles? Where was Walt frozen? Dairy Queen?

In short—and I was very short—I was making a name for myself. It wasn't necessarily a good name, but as the saying goes: as long as they spell your name right . . .

"Duane's a fag!" was scrawled in Magic Marker on my locker door the following day. Even the effeminate Mickey Mouse didn't get such treatment . . . and Minnie Mouse? Please. What a beard! So it wasn't exactly my name up in lights. However, furthering the marketing motto: any publicity . . .

By my senior year—not that you're asking—I gave up. I was blowing this pop stand and never looking back.

Now, high school has been compared to so many levels of life, most of them terrible. It's a distilled experience of economic division, racism, sexism, ethnic cleansing, homophobia, and an overdose of hormones. And that's just during PE.

American culture has always been obsessed with the jocks and the cheerleaders, but it's most often the heavy girls and the skinny nerds who become class valedictorian or the first dot-com billionaire at the class reunion held at any random Ramada Inn. There is also a wild parallel between the number of arrests, imprisonments, second/third marriages, rehab stays, suicides, and bad toupees. But enough about Ridgewood, class of '77.

During those school years, it seemed I spent more time inside my locker than out. And those confinements were almost always the work of one particular boy: one raffishly handsome, abusively curious, seductively mean, rough trade-ready boy/man. We had a gym class together, the only class we ever shared, as I was in the nerdy, smart-kid group where dreams went to die . . . and die young. He, on the other strong mitt, was in "D group," which was a notch above special education and twice as unpredictable. While they were throwing food, he was throwing the fire alarm.

After one rather confusing game of touch football, I was pummeled by my own teammates. Oh yes, I did run with the ball in the wrong direction and scored for the opposing team. That day, everyone beat the crap out of me. In the boy's locker room, the lockers were too small for even my diminutive frame to now be squeezed inside. My studly nemesis was forced to devise an alternative plan of attack.

Within seconds, this six-foot-three-inch slab of jutting arms and legs had pinned me to the floor; he was on top of me, and I couldn't move a scrawny muscle as his hands held me in place, our faces inches apart. His voice had a white trash twang inconsistent with our heavily Polish and Italian neighborhood, but that made him all the more appealing to my eager ears. He hung above me Sistine Chapel–like, and I could only look up into his big, dumb, striking mug, those beagle-dog brown eyes, his large, off-kilter Roman nose, his lazy snarl. I knew he was going to strike me, yet I almost melted.

Mirroring my strict Catholic upbringing, I'm stretched Christlike on the floor, held down by a would-be Roman soldier himself . . . if he even knew what or where Rome was. Now I'm lost somewhere amid the shouted abuse of odd non sequiturs, as if warming up for some maladjusted bully's roast. I wiggled and squirmed, but I never let on that of all the people who beat me up—and yes, I did keep a list—he was my favorite. Strike me to hell for my next thought: *If you have to be beaten, let it be by the beautiful.*

As his screed continued, I realized we've never been horizontal before. I hardly encouraged this situation, but here we were. Like a butterfly pinned to the board, unable to move or save myself, my inner caterpillar suddenly hatched a most dangerous thought: *What if I just . . . ?* His hands held me even tighter; the muscled weight of his body pressed me against the cold tile floor, and there was nowhere to go but up.

In a fast, forceful lunge, I quickly pulled up my head—the only part of me I could move—and I spit smack kissed that wide mouth full and as hard and wet and as long as I possibly could. I stayed there for what seemed like an endlessly lazy forever. But my dear abuser, still in his four-point position, had nowhere to go, momentarily at least. It would be near impossible for him to jump straight up from such an awkward stance.

And the kiss, that hard vengeful kiss, stunned the boy like no sting ever could. We both just hung there in the air for a second or three . . . both somehow frozen in the coupling, he most uncomfortable and me, um, mostly not. In the following breathless seconds, the beautiful boy rolled off of me, mumbling, "What the fuck?" He fell away, his sizable erection most visible. If there were witnesses to this faux rape, I can only envision them holding Olympic placards: 8.5, 9.0, 9.5. Perhaps these were scores. Perhaps they were measurements.

I rolled in the opposite direction and ran from the locker room, certain he was going to kill me. But he didn't follow. Strange.

A week later, he approached me in the hallway with his usual posse. As he put his big mitts around me, I tried to shake off the thought of what was to come. "This is my little buddy!" he announced to his friends. "No one touches him. Ever!"

WTF?

And that was the last time I was beaten up in high school. Over the next year, my beautiful boy would, on occasion, toss that same muscular arm around my skittish shoulder. He'd ask me how I was doing, and if anyone was bothering me, I should let him know. Every time, he would call me his "little buddy." I don't know why. But after that one weird smooch, I was somehow off limits to the abuse of others. Fuck, this sexy bully had clout.

Today, I realize what I did was exceptionally dangerous, and I don't suggest it to anyone caught in a similar situation. Yes, people have been killed for less. I felt trapped and reacted . . . or overreacted. And I was very lucky.

Somehow, there was more to this abuse than I'd realized at the time. Somewhere in that moment, we both discovered something unique within ourselves. For me, I found my first taste of courage, if a kiss can be courageous. For him . . . well, perhaps it was his first flirtation with true affection.

Over fifty years have now passed, in which I've heard many stories about my beautiful boy's life: his parent's divorce as a child and that he never did finish high school, the girl he got pregnant and his drug problems and troubles with the law. A tough life.

I think often about those beagle-dog brown eyes and that lazy snarl. I think of that lost affection, that one slender instance found and the hold that kept us briefly bound. Gone. As if it hardly ever was. But together, in that one single kiss, was the most freeing moment we would ever share.

CHAPTER 7

OSCAR, OSCAR, OSCAR

Scene One

Marge put down the breakfast bowls for her five cats, but only three of the little furry ones zigzagged about her ankles in full-throated meowing mode. She called out for the remaining MIA two and then started a pot of coffee. It would prove to be the beginning of a very long day.

Her husband, Jack, whose body was not in the freezer as she so often joked to her tag sale buddies, clomped into the kitchen, his slippers slipping past one ravenous feline who was intent on eating every other kitty's food. "One day, that cat's gonna explode," Jack groggily announced as he stood before the coffee maker, monogrammed souvenir Niagara Falls mug in hand. "And I ain't cleanin' that up!"

Marge dropped two slices of bread into her pristine Sunbeam toaster. "Then we'll get another," she replied. "I'm turning down kittens as often as I do estate sale clients."

The two stood quietly with only the wolfing sound of feeding felines cutting through their 1950s kitchen, the metal cabinets providing a soft echo to the kibble-chewing cracks.

Jack released a long sigh. "I don't think I can do this anymore," he complained. "It's all . . . well, it's really getting to me."

The toast and Marge simultaneously popped. "Ugh, this again?" With a bitter hand, she began spreading the marmalade she had discovered at the previous weekend's farmer's market.

"Hey, watch it!" Jack said, snapping his toast from her. "It's just toast, Marge, not the Ripper murders."

Marge threw the knife into a sink full of dirty dishes. "You're gonna be toast if you're starting up with this shit again. I've told you before: If you're done, quit. If you're not, quit your bitching!"

Jack pulled back a '50s chrome kitchen chair and sat down at the fire-engine red dinette set he had rescued from the neighbor's garage sale. "I'm not saying this wasn't fun in the beginning, because it was. But Jesus,

Marge, I started this almost ten years ago. Things have changed. I've changed."

"You took early retirement to do this, remember?" Marge dropped barely a tablespoon of milk into a chipped Russell Wright coffee cup and sat opposite Jack. She started to reach for his hand, but he flinched, nervously pulling it back.

Molly, the suspected bulimic cat, now began her clockwork-like retching sounds: the one, two, three puke of it all projectile vomiting across the kitchen floor, barely missing another cat's late arrival to breakfast.

"You're kidding me!" Marge said in frustration.

Jack brushed it off. "Oh, that cat pukes every morning."

Marge barked back, "No, not the damn cat. You! If you don't want to sell online anymore, then stop. I mean, we still need the money—I've no idea how that fact has slipped your mind, but fine. Quit, and then you can stop complaining about it. But you damn well better have a plan B, cuz your wife here thinks you're being an a-hole!"

Jack bristled, recalling the countless times this discussion had been rehashed with no resolution in sight. After a considerable silence—the only sound heard being Molly the cat contentedly eating yet another cat's meal—Jack once again attempted to make his case. "It's the customers, if you can call them that. I'm just tired,

Marge, of the returns, the refunds, the ridiculous emails, the cheapness, and yes, the crookedness of some people. It's exhausting. I have my pride, you know. I pride myself on being reputable. Heck, my ratings and reviews prove that. But it's nearly impossible to stay positive—and let's be honest, profitable—when it's two sales forward, one sale back."

Frustrated, he jumped from his chair. "Just wait here," he continued. "I've gotta show you this email."

Marge began wiping up the cat barf and had mostly finished by the time Jack returned, waving a piece of paper in his sticky marmalade fingers. "This motherf'er . . ." he began, "bought a lobby card from me—one of the scarcer cards from *Gone with the Wind*. He needled me down on the price over more emails than I can count and gets his free shipping, whatever. You can see where this is going, right? He gets it and then claims it's a reprint—and Marge, come on, I've been doing this for decades. I know a reprint when I see it, and he tells me he's returning it. And what does he send me back? An actual fucking reprint! I can show you the stock of paper it's printed on, and it's not the original I sent him. No, that he keeps and sticks me with his garbage!" Jack's face is now as red as their kitchen table, the veins rising out on his forehead.

Marge grabs his hand again, this time successful, and holds it in hers. "Okay, first, relax. This isn't the first asshole, and he won't be the last. Contact eBay and tell them what happened. As God as my witness, you'll never be happy until you report him."

Jack half smiled. "A *Gone with the Wind* joke? And a bad one at that . . ."

"Hey, it's early," she replied, releasing his hand and replacing it with a coffee pot for another round of caffeine. "It's all I got."

He shook his head and finished his toast. "Open another eBay claim, I know. But this is what I'm up against: fighting with customers—and I use the term loosely—and then with eBay. Yeah, I'll figure it out, but this sort of thing only used to happen once or twice a year. I swear, now it's almost monthly. Not this identical scam, but similar. People claiming they never received an item even though it was signed for at delivery. People ordering something then denying it or blaming their kid for hacking their account. Or how about the guy who took a microscope—a freaking *microscope*, Marge—to a vintage Tod Browning's Freaks poster to claim there was fold damage. Fold damage! You know me: my listings are anally, neurotically accurate when it comes to an item's condition. As if a poster from 1932 was never ever folded? Fuck me!"

Marge took a slow sip of her coffee and swallowed her husband's all-too-often-repeated complaints. "Would this help matters?" she said softly.

"What?" Jack replied, still riled up from his own monologue.

"If I fucked you," she said flatly.

"Oh God! That's probably the worst line of seduction I've ever heard."

Marge turned away. "Hey, maybe after thirty-five years of marriage, eBay resolution isn't much of an aphrodisiac. Work with me here. You're stressed; I'm stressed. It's just a thought."

Standing behind her, Jack gently began to massage her tightening shoulders and then leaned down to her ear. "Thank you," he said softly. "Think I can get a rain check?"

Marge reached back and squeezed the hand on her loosening muscle. "Sure, sure. It's not like it's ever monsoon season in this house."

It was a tender moment until Molly spit up her second breakfast.

Scene Two

The following day was a busy one for Marge, with two estate-sale pitches to make in as many hours, a close craziness in terms of scheduling. Her first was in the village of Skokie at the home of an elderly Jewish man who had moved into an assisted living facility. The second was in the upscale town of Park Ridge, where someone's aunt had died of COVID. With her husband's early morning complaints still in her head, she wasn't looking forward to either one.

The Skokie job seemed promising, with the family seemingly motivated to clear out the contents of the house with as little grief as possible. It was a cute two-bedroom bungalow with a clean basement, garage, and a broom-swept attic. The man's wife had died the year before, and the family had already made an efficient pass through the house, removing whatever heirlooms they deemed most important. Marge made what she felt was a fair appraisal of most of the home's contents and her commensurate fee. *Next!*

After a mad dash through suburban Chicago traffic, she arrived in Park Ridge, an interesting if somewhat snooty suburb. She'd not had a sale in the area before, and at first glance, it felt like the elevated north shore mannerisms of an upscale Kenilworth without the matching money. Not that the home—or for that matter, the neighborhood—wasn't nice. It was. However, there was something Marge couldn't place her vintage-acquiring finger on; something felt, well, off. Just not well-off.

Still, like the potential Skokie sale, it was a lovely, well-kept home with a family that appeared prepared for what needed to be done. With iPad in hand, she ventured from room to well-stocked room, documenting the inventory stars (and turds) from basement to attic. She had nearly completed her appraisal when the niece of the deceased beckoned her over to a locked display case.

"There's just one more item here you may find of interest," the niece offered. "I've no idea how my aunt acquired it, maybe from one of her many husbands." She laughed. "Turns out she was as good of a bride as she was a widow . . . times four!"

Marge's eye grew Little Orphan Annie wide as the woman opened the glass showcase and handed her a golden object.

"I believe these were made in Chicago, perhaps still are? At least that's all I've been able to discover." The niece let out a nervous giggle. "God bless the internet!"

Shaking, Marge held the heavy object, turning it over and over again in disbelief. "However did you—"

The niece cut her off. "I don't know. But my aunt had it displayed right here in this showcase for, seemingly, ever. I remember it from my childhood. I mean, she'd never let us play with it. God forbid, right?"

It was an Oscar, a pristine and dazzling Academy Award statuette. Now, for the purposes of this true story, let's just say it was for "Mary Somebody." Or as Jack would later jest, "Mary Anybody," as this particular award-winning actress wasn't exactly the pretty one.

Marge, failing her attempt at calm composure, knew she had to buy this prized Academy Award. Poor Jack had been in such a bad mood as of late; how could this most impossible-to-find treasure not make him beyond happy? As a Hollywood memorabilia dealer and collector, it was the Holy Grail and just as golden.

Setting aside a lifetime of ethics as the owner of a well-regarded estate sale company, the previously unthinkable words that come out of Marge's mouth next surprised even her: "Would you sell this directly to me today? As in, right here, right now? My husband, well, he's a serious collector, and I promise he'll never resell it—this is for his personal collection."

Without missing a beat, the woman shot back, "How much?"

Marge was surprised by the response but also encouraged. *She's going to sell this to me,* she thought. *I just know it.* So Marge turned to what she did best: blunt honesty.

"Listen," she began, "an item like this is, putting it mildly, is a double-edged sword. Everyone is going to want to buy it, but the publicity can go either way. I'm not sure you're even legally permitted to sell it; I mean, I seem to recall something about that in the press. But sold privately, well . . . Who's to know, right?

The woman thought for a moment then replied with an efficiently repeated: "So how much?"

"A thousand dollars," Marge countered without hesitation. "Cash. Today."

"Whatever would I do with the darn thing anyway?" the woman asked, more to herself than to Marge. "I mean, I guess that seems fair. Cash, right?"

Marge embraced the Oscar like she had won the best supporting actress award at an estate sale, holding it to her breast and coveting her good fortune. Within the hour, she made a run to the ATM and, combining that with a few hundred emergency dollars she kept stashed in her bag, the deal was done.

Driving home from the transaction, Marge mentally thanked the Academy, all those little people out there in the dark, and those smiling-down resale gods. Life was good.

Scene Three

Marge didn't get the Skokie job. "Somebody knew somebody," and the family decided to go with a firm better connected to charitable Jewish thrifts. No matter. Marge never countered when a religious organization was in the picture. To her, in the end, someone eventually had to pay retail.

Still, the better news arrived that the estate of little Miss Nobody's statuette had been awarded to Marge: maybe the odd, if not inappropriate, transaction had paved the way for the contract's signing and the successful sale of the home's content. Happy family, mostly happy buyers, and most of all, a very happy Jack.

The Oscar now held a rarified place of honor in Jack's home office between a pair of Egyptian book-ends and the urn holding the ashes of their first cat, Mr. Claus.

Over the last few months, there had rarely been a week when Jack didn't mention Marge's special gift to him. In fact, a few "rain checks" were even cashed during that time, making the days perhaps a bit less stressful, if not peaceful. Maybe just a little bit of Hollywood magic had been sprinkled into their home; Lord knows they needed it.

Trouble, so the saying goes, seems to come in threes, and the impending situation would be no different. It began, unbeknownst to Marge, with persistent, if not pestering messages sent to Jack. In his defense, he should have kept his big yapper shut, but in his excitement in owning something very few people would ever be lucky enough to acquire, he let the cat—and not one of their five—out of the bag. Yes, he blabbed to some Facebook "friend" of his wife's great Oscar find.

The second round of trouble began with the emails escalating into telephone calls, some at all hours of the sleepless nights. Jack could not keep them secret for long as his loud responses to the stranger on the phone echoed within Marge's earshot. "No, it's not for sale, like I've told you before. Please stop calling!" Et cetera.

Marge was livid. Stay out all night with the boys. Buy out another estate of Hollywood memorabilia that the both of them would never live long enough to sell. Shit, have an affair with some bimbo. But blab about his wife's big score? That could be a costly mistake.

"Jesus, Mary, and give-me-a-break Joseph, why did you have to mention anything about the Oscar?"

"I only told one person," he mumbled as he sat on the edge of the bed, smartphone in hand.

"One person," repeated Marge, "is like six degrees of chlamydia. Now everyone's infected."

"Maybe he'll stop calling."

But he—whoever he was—didn't. The calls continued for another week. Finally, while Jack was in an extended bathroom visit (see: bladder over sixty), Marge answered his phone on the nightstand. It started off pleasantly enough, but the soft-spoken man on the other end was surprised to hear a female voice, and it quickly became threatening. The stranger's demand: sell him the Oscar or he would call the police.

Marge waited until he had completed his rather "gone with the long-winded" threat before offering her response: "Listen, asswipe. I don't know who you are, who you *think* you are, or who you think you're going to be, but if you call this number again, you're a dead man! Got it? If you come near my home, I'll chop your dick off and feed it to my cats. Not that it'd be much of a snack, you piece of shit!"

Click.

Round three began the following day when a pair of detectives arrived at their door asking about the hot Oscar. Both Marge and Jack countered with their story of receiving the stalker's Facebook messages and phone calls, but the officers were nonplussed. It seemed odd they would take the word of a stranger over theirs, but then perhaps they didn't have the entire Hollywood picture.

While the two officers said they'd be back with a search warrant, Jack expressed his concern about the determined telephonic collector. Police and firemen were often manically serious collectors of police and fire memorabilia; his experience told him they would skirt the law, if not break it, to snag a most desirable badge, hat, uniform, or other related rarity.

What if the same were true of their present predicament? Maybe this Oscar-demanding guy had connections; maybe he was the detective's nephew. Fuck, maybe it was one of the detectives himself.

The next day was a Saturday, and Marge was up early to host her next estate sale. Jack, finishing up a shave, was barely dressed when the doorbell rang. Marge stumbled over multiple cats to the door and opened to the same two detectives, warrant in hand.

"Well, fuck me!" she exclaimed.

"Pardon?" said the detective. Marge accepted the warrant and stepped aside. As Jack walked into the room, buttoning his shirt, the first detective began scouring the house. The second started to explain the nature of the warrant, but Jack just shut him down with, "It's here in my office," while directing the man down the small hallway. "On the shelf . . . next to the dead cat."

The detective returned with the Oscar in question, and within moments, Jack found himself handcuffed and being led out the door. He only had time to shout the words "eBay resolution!" from halfway down the driveway.

Marge was stunned, a condition she rarely found herself in given her expertise at many a shit show of an estate sale. "You gotta be kidding me," she mumbled half to herself, but it was too late. The joke was now on her.

Within the hour, Marge called her estate sales team and made some baloney excuse about her car, her cats, or that the cats can't drive a car . . . she didn't really remember exactly what she told them other than they needed to conduct the morning sale without her. At the police station, she was told that since it was Saturday, no judge would be hearing the matter until the following Monday when bail would be set. Jack now needed to "sit his ass in jail for the weekend." The detective's words, not hers.

The drive home was long and tear-filled. While she blamed Jack for this mess, had she not started it all? The most perfect gift was now a litigious mess. She thought of the words of her mother-in-law: "The road to hell is paved with good intentions." *Yes,* she thought as she pulled into the asphalt driveway, *it is. That and assholes!*

As long as the trip home had been, the weekend was even longer; a Jackless house was quieter than she could stand. His complaining, though greatly reduced these past months, was now sorely missed. Marge found herself picking up her cats and hugging them as bitterly wriggling babies. She didn't even feel the claw marks running up and down her arms—she was that numb.

Jack was allowed to call her once on Sunday, and though the conversation was brief, she learned that the food was terrible and he was the best-looking guy in there, whatever that meant. Mostly they talked about the hearing on the following day. Oddly, he seemed in better spirits than her. Maybe his expertise in old Hollywood prison films had better prepared him for his weekend's sojourn. Maybe her interest in the rerunning of nearly any Bette Davis movie had girded her loins, if not prepared her for a bumpy night or two.

Come Monday, Marge found herself seated in the early morning courtroom of some obscure judge. She thought about all the times she had near unconsciously voted for judges at the ballot box with nary an idea of their skills, qualifications, or city hall connections. Now, however, they were experiencing the great tossing of the legal dice, a courtroom where anything could, and often did, happen.

A public defender sidled up to Marge, saying, "I read up on the charges, not to worry. I'll have Jack out on bail before lunch. Oh, and the special at the civic center's cafeteria is Mongolian chicken, should you be so interested." She was not.

To Marge's relief, a female judge soon appeared, which inexplicably calmed her nerves, as if this sad Hollywood story would somehow strike a female magistrate with greater sympathy. Jack's case was the fourth on the docket, so after a series of equally semiserious cases—DUI, trespassing, a flashing indecent exposure, and someone who stuffed a French bulldog puppy down his pants and was busted in the Petco parking lot—Jack's case was finally called.

A faceless district attorney read the charge and editorialized on Jack's flagrant disregard of the law. The judge flipped some pages and asked the public defender, "How does the defendant plead?"

But before the man could even stand, Jack jumped up and yelled, "Not guilty, Your Honor!"

"No, no, no!" said the public defender and Marge simultaneously.

"Not guilty," Jack repeated.

The judge looked over her glasses; this was not her first rodeo or her sighting of a horse's ass. "Sir," she began, "you were found in possession of a stolen item, were you not?" Jack nodded. "And I'm holding both a search warrant and one for your arrest, am I not?"

He nodded again.

"Well, I'll make this very easy," she stated flatly. "Just tell us how you found yourself in possession of the Oscar, and we can settle this very quickly. But I warn you: don't waste the court's time, or this may not be pleasant for you."

Marge suddenly felt herself pale into whiteness. Explaining to the judge what had happened or, worse still, revealing the true owner would be the third rail of resale. Over the years, she had found herself in only a few similarly messy situations: accidentally selling something that had not been for sale or, equally awful, the family changed their mind and wanted a sold item returned—all the stuff of resale nightmares.

Reputations hung precariously on how matters like these were resolved or not resolved. But Marge could not bring a closed estate into *this* boondoggle; to be honest with both the court and herself, her hands were unclean.

Jack stared at her with an intense knowingness of not only his problem but hers as well. He had to do something—and quick. "Your Honor," he began, "may I ask you a question?"

The judge blinked. "This court is not here to answer your questions, sir."

But Jack continued. "Are you familiar with the actress in question—the one who won this particular Academy Award?"

"I don't see what . . ."

"You see, Your Honor, her award was a bit of a fluke. If you look at her filmography, to be kind, there's quite a few of stinkers in there."

The district attorney and public defender each let out a contained snicker, and the judge gaveled them both. "Can you get to the point?" She exhaled.

"If I may, Your Honor. The actress who received this award was more surprised than anyone. If you google it, you'll see what I'm saying is true. And my purchase of this Oscar, I will admit, was a terrible mistake. But also a bit of a fluke."

The judge pulled her glasses back up onto her nose and reviewed the charging documents. A long, anguished-filled moment passed while she seemed to consider something, perhaps relevant or irrelevant, to the case. Or maybe she had a sudden taste for Mongolian chicken.

Setting the charging documents aside, she began: "When I saw your case on the docket this morning, I did some research of my own. A stolen Academy Award . . . well, it can be a messy topic regarding ownership.

You certainly didn't win it—we know that for certain. And I'm not about to open up a kettle of fish that'll stink up my courtroom today, sir. So I'm going to ask you straight out: Will you change your plea to guilty if the court agrees not to pursue the originating ownership of this Oscar?" Then much louder, "And before you answer, you need to know that there will not be another remedy offered by this court."

Marge swallowed so hard Jack could have tasted it.

"I do, Your Honor." Jack sighed in relief. "I absolutely plead guilty under those terms."

Now the final credits were about to roll with the judge proclaiming: "By order of this court, the Oscar statuette will be returned to the Academy of Motion Picture Arts and Sciences and the defendant released upon the payment of a fine of one thousand dollars. Case dismissed."

When the gavel hit the bench, Marge jumped out of her seat. As Jack was being led from the courtroom, he yelled, "A thousand bucks, honey; it's like eBay resolution!"

Later that night, Jack and Marge celebrated their good fortune with a bottle of champagne and five chipped Fiesta bowls of milk.

CHAPTER 8

BEFORE AND AFTER

Should you ever find yourself in the spotlight glare of major media exposure, perhaps the following true story will give you pause for thought. For me, it was rather puzzling.

A few years ago, I was approached about appearing on a particular segment of a major cable television show. At the time, it was number one in its time slot, I was told: "It's the opportunity of a lifetime." Yes, it had a huge audience, and this fact was dangled before me like a carrot in front of a dizzy donkey.

Of course, like a jackass, I bit.

The premise of my proposed segment was a simple one: an antiques expert would be brought into my store (a vintage specialist), and she would point out fake Bakelite jewelry: brooches, pins, necklaces, etc.

To contrast this scam, she would have with her—oh so conveniently—real Bakelite pieces with which to compare.

After the shock of this confusing concept wore off, I pointed out that I didn't sell fake Bakelite or anything else I knew was a reproduction. Still, I was told, "*Tsk-tsk. Not to worry.*" The producers would gladly plant fake pieces within my store so their expert could "find" such faux troublemakers and demonstrate to the audience the joys and cautionary woes of collecting early plastic phenolic resins.

Their thoughtfulness underwhelmed me.

Apparently, my part in this scheming television segment, should I choose to accept, was the role of the potential pitfall, the bad boy of Bakelite, the faux fool. Not exactly something one would put on a resume or a loan application. Try calling your mother to tell her you'll be on television as the flimflam artist in the trench coat and dark sunglasses.

Almost facetiously, I asked how it would come across to the audience at home. Would the show not be implying to the viewers that I knowingly sold reproductions? If so, would that not only be a serious falsehood but damaging to my good name and reputation?

"*Tut-tut.* Not to worry!" the producers cooed once again. They saw absolutely no problems or potential downside for me whatsoever. In fact, I was to stand directly beside their expert and contribute my commentary, whatever that might be. How impossibly wrong could this go, right?

Exhibit A

Expert: "What we can see quite clearly here in this reproduction is its lack of weight, the poor quality of the carving, and its overall lack of genuineness. In truth, it sickens me to even be holding this item in my hand. Can someone please get me a wet nap?"

Me (stuttering): "Um, that's not mine! I've never seen that piece before in my life. It's a setup, see? I was duped. I'm a patsy, I tell you. A patsy!"

(A gunshot is heard.)

Expert: "This is why you should always know who you're buying from. And not from this person presently standing beside me nervously exuding flop sweat."

Overdramatized a bit, yes. But you can see the impending dilemma. If this had been live television, perhaps I would have had a fighting chance. I could have blown the cover of this retro ruse, tried to make a lame joke, or inserted a hot pin into this expert to determine whether he/she was a "real" expert or not. At least that's how they do it in my acupuncturist's office.

Unfortunately, this show was to be taped, and the editing was out of my hands. In essence, I was throwing the truth . . . and my real Bakelite jewelry . . . out the vintage window. What were my chances of realistic objectivity in this opportunity other than looking like the aforementioned ass?

After much soul-searching, I finally made my decision and approached the producers with my best revelatory explanation. Drumroll, please: "No one ever wants to be the 'before' picture—in anything. Everyone wants to be the 'after' photo."

In "after," there is always the promise or at least the possibility of satisfaction. Things are always looking up for after. Things are good. "After" routinely gets the girl or boy and sometimes both. Damn, "after" is good!

But "before"? Ugh, what a mess. Where do we even start? He's the old joke: the day his ship comes in, he'll be at the train station. And it'll be the day . . . before! Face it: "before" is a loser and completely unfuckable. There, I've said it and done all you "before" people a huge favor. Now the truth will set you free to get a decent haircut. And have someone look at your teeth while you're at it. This "before" look of yours is so . . . yesterday.

I had to repeat variations on this simple theme innumerable times until it finally began to sink into their addled cable-programming brains. Still, they were completely confused by my comparisons and rambled on about the tremendous exposure, the incredible opportunity, the terrible mistake I was about to make. My favorite was: "No one ever turns us down," said in a very menacing Donald Trump/Darth Vader tone.

My friends thought I was absolutely insane/stupid for turning down this supposed golden opportunity. For days, I heard a perpetual chorus of "But there has to be a way to do this! Think of a way . . . think!"

But there wasn't. That was the offer. This was the deal, and their big offer was a platform . . . from which, apparently, I could jump off. I was lucky this wasn't being filmed at the end of a dock.

In the end, I passed on the segment and show. The producers repeatedly cried, "But *no one* turns us down."

And I had a most satisfactory reply: "Now you can stop saying that, because someone just did."

It killed me, it really did, but I did learn a few valuable life lessons:

1. Just because you *can* do something doesn't mean you always *should*.

2. If you can avoid making a complete ass of yourself, don't miss that opportunity.

3. Unless you can catch a bullet in your teeth, steer clear of media gunplay.

Epilogue: Not only did this horrible segment never find a suitable replacement faux fall guy, the entire concept was ultimately dropped. I may have missed my fifteen minutes of uncomfortable fame, but I don't think I missed much. Well, not much that was real, anyway.

CHAPTER 9

THE LOST SUPERSTAR

I have debated for decades about relating this story for reasons soon to become obvious. I could easily slip into a tawdry tale that would read more like an excerpt from the screenplay of Al Pacino's *Cruising* than Jack and Ennis's love story in *Brokeback Mountain*. No, my story—and that of the gentleman in question—falls somewhere most comfortably, most seductively, and, dare I say, most romantically in the middle.

I met Paul at a Chicago bar in 1981. Initially, I didn't know anything about him other than his first name; in fact, he didn't even mention his last name until much later in our assignation. His voice was soft, his manner gentle, and he was one of the sexiest men I had ever met. Movie star handsome, masculine, and fuzzy faced in the most meticulous of ways, his eyes could melt the ice cubes in your glass. He certainly did mine.

Initially, I assumed he was a model or an actor—he was too strikingly handsome to not be caught up in either profession. He was dirty blond beautiful but far from dumb, having a country boy swag infused with a big city wit that was totally disarming and hypnotically charming. As we chatted, he looked at me with long, thoughtful stares that one cannot help but fall into. And fast. In that first meeting, he mentioned he was passing through Chicago to visit a friend and he currently lived in a commune in Indiana.

Paul knew he was attractive—he'd spent a lifetime being told so—but he was dismissive, almost embarrassed about the matter when a compliment fell his way. I flattered the tousle of his blond locks, and he just said: "Thanks!" I immediately learned not to do that again.

We chatted for hours, buying each other drinks and ignoring almost everyone else in the room. The bartender dawdled over us, well, at least over Paul. The late afternoon turned into early evening, and though we talked about many things, notably Chicago vs. New York, the respective comparative qualities of topics as diverse as theatre and pizza, he gave me nothing of a personal nature.

Finally, toward the end of cocktail round three or four, he turned to me and asked quite simply, "Have you ever heard of Paul America?"

"Oh yes," I said, still thinking we were small talking. I did not immediately make the right-before-my-eyes connection. "He's one of those Warhol people, right? Edie Sedgwick, *Ciao! Manhattan?*"

He seemed to flinch at the 1972 film reference and then quietly replied: "Well, he used to be me."

I'm still shocked that I didn't fall off my barstool after hearing that statement.

Perhaps a bit of backstory is required here: In the mid-1960s, Andy Warhol decided to establish his own studio system as part of his "Factory" live/work space to create art and different forms of media. He called his discoveries his "superstars," inspired from the golden age of the Hollywood's studio system. Today, the late Edie Sedgwick is most often remembered as the icon of that decade; however, she was not the first star in Warhol's galaxy.

The early stars launched at the Factory during Warhol's first forays into film were performers such as Viva, Ultra Violet, Ondine, Candy Darling, Brigid Berlin, Holly Woodlawn—some were actual women, some trans-sexuals, some transvestites. Warhol reintroduced the cinematic "drag queen" to a mainstream audience on a scale never before exposed.

But Warhol's first male superstar, an impossibly handsome and 100 percent masculine star, was the gentleman now seated beside me, Paul America.

Later, other male performers, such as übersexy Joe Dallesandro, would be rolled out in starring feature films of their own, but it was Paul America who broke Factory ground. Sadly, and as is often the case, Paul would not be the trailblazer who gained the glory.

Legend has it that Paul's residential occupancy at the America Hotel in NYC originally sparked his new last name. Borrowing another page from the studio system in which Roy Scherer became Rock Hudson (Rock of Gibraltar/Hudson River), Paul Johnson became Paul America.

With his all-American good looks, America would quickly become the first male Warhol superstar with the classic *My Hustler* (1965). Though Warhol promised much, he delivered less, and assorted proposed sequels never saw the light of day.

And Paul never saw a dime.

In retrospect, the world wasn't quite ready for a gay male lead. He wasn't campy, lisping, or an effeminate queen. On the contrary: Paul was masculine sexy, hirsute hairy, and decidedly more bisexual—a word we still seem unwilling to fully embrace—both on-screen and off.

Paul appeared in the silent art film *Harold* with Edie Sedgwick about the artist Harold Stephenson; there's not much to the film save them all lounging about on a couch without purpose. In a nutshell, this was rather the problem: more often than not, Paul was used as a prop or part of the scenery; his acting talent was always somehow diminished at the director's hand.

He also appeared briefly in the documentary short *Superartist* (1967), but again, more of Paul America seemed to end up on the cutting room floor. The problem was that in an era of flashy and sadly campy drag queens, there was little air left in the room for Paul to grow and be seen. He was a second banana when there was little interest in bananas, sexy or not. Paul was a good actor put in consistently bad situations.

Not wanting to be a one-hit wonder, Paul was serious about his acting and appeared in the now classic *Ciao! Manhattan*. Rumors persisted that he and Edie Sedgwick were "crazy in love," and I believe this was true. Like the gender fluidity of today, Paul didn't label himself straight or gay, although his gay fan base kept *My Hustler* running in art houses for many years. Paul was beautiful to both the eye and to the camera, and one can certainly see a young Edie being smitten by the attentions of his smoldering good looks, if not his fragile fuzziness.

It is well-documented that perhaps the most famous footnote of Paul's legacy was his intervention in a number of Edie Sedgwick's early overdoses. Sadly, he wasn't at her last.

In the years that followed, Hollywood would shun Paul, his Factory pedigree not opening a single door. Serious industry decision-makers cared little for Warhol's superstars and the drugs that followed many of them to early graves. For Paul, East Coast fame never transferred any farther west than midnight showings of his films at San Francisco's Castro Theatre.

His one hit, *My Hustler*, typecast him in a real-life role that he did not accept. Paul America was not a hustler, although he certainly could have been, had he so chosen. He was a promising young actor and might have been the next smoldering James Dean or tightly wound Sal Mineo. Paul's unfulfilled promise was a loss to us all. By our modern measure, Paul America was the precursor to Heath Ledger; for a brief moment in time, he was adored by men and women alike and then gone too soon.

A few short months after our lazy afternoon and a most memorable evening, Paul America was struck by a car and killed while walking home from his dentist's office in Ormond Beach, Florida. He was just thirty-eight years old. His death was scarcely noted by the press, and the legacy of Paul America, cult icon, passed into oblivion.

Sadly, few knew he had died. Like Elvis, there were Paul America sightings from time to time, rumors of another film, a cable television show. In fact, he'd been dead for years. It was only with the advent of the internet and a continually inaccurate Wikipedia page (which for years implied he was still alive) that it became clear

Paul left us long ago. Today, Paul America is a footnote to Warhol's vast legacy—rather a vintage victim to fame and a time so tragically limited, his life cut short by a cruel twist of circumstances, not unlike the demise of Warhol himself in 1987.

Paul had his flaws . . . the rampant drug use, his disappearing acts, and too frequent arrests, but he actually fared well in a decade of overdoses and suicides, especially being birthed in the Factory stable. To his credit, he somehow found a path to survive that experience.

In what would be our last moment together, he hesitatingly reminisced about his life, seemingly speaking more to the heavens than to me. Still, I listened, safely satiated in his arms.

"Someday," I sighed, "you need to tell your story."

"Nah," he countered in a slow drawl, gently rubbing his hand across my bristly buzzcut. "They only want Warhol. And that's okay."

He was right about that back then, but it's still so wrong.

Now when I close my eyes and dream back to those lazy hours, I can still see his handsome face, feel his gentle spirit, fall intoxicated with the promise of what love could be . . . he was that easy to love . . .

Of course, I now recognize I probably meant little to Paul America, and that's okay too. Perhaps I had the kismet of meeting him those many decades ago so I could honor him now in this delicate memory, which otherwise could not have been told.

Perhaps within this confidence, there rests a certain honor that I alone can share.

I think that like so many of us—famous, infamous, and everyone in-between—Paul America was happiest when someone simply cared. I know I still do.

And maybe in the end, that's all that really matters.

CHAPTER 10

1937: HORIZON ON A PRAYER

Beyond the possessions of their estate, one of the most significant things you can purchase from a dead person is their home. The sheer scale of the transaction, both in size and financial outlay, diminishes the scale of almost anything else you could possibly buy. While real estate brokers and home inspectors search for foundation cracks and leaking basement walls, the vintage buyer seeks out walls that talk: the chatterboxes are always best.

In 2005, I was fortunate to acquire a tiny fourth-floor co-op in New York's Greenwich Village. It had been a lifelong dream to move to Manhattan, but my vintage retail business was thriving, so permanently relocating was out of the question. I had too many Chicago irons in the fire to risk getting burned by my own inattentiveness.

But I'm getting ahead of myself . . .

For years before my real estate purchase, my monthly jaunts to New York City to sell at the venerable Pier Antique Shows, shop the Midtown flea markets, see a few Broadway shows, or just goof off had become, quite honestly, astronomically costly. This expense was the primary reason I needed to buy an apartment and stop wasting money on hotel rooms. I would save myself some hard-earned bacon, nitrates be damned.

On the grid-worn path to becoming a NYC home-owner, I had always searched out the cheapest, and often most vile, Manhattan hotels imaginable in order to afford my nomadic vintage NYC lifestyle. I stayed in hotels so disgusting, they'd have required extensive remodeling before anyone would even consider commit-ting suicide in their rooms. I certainly wasn't about to slit my wrists in a filthy bathroom sink or hang myself from a dirty shower curtain. I wouldn't have cared if a drag Anthony Perkins were cleaning my bath; just put some elbow grease into scrubbing that bloody tub, woman!

True story: I once scored an extremely cheap hotel room in Chinatown only because the management couldn't completely remove the "666" painted above the bed, the chalk outline of a body having cleaned up ever so nicely from a few days earlier.

I may be Bohemian by birth, but even I couldn't get too artsy-crafty with those hypodermic needles scattered in the closet. And where's Martha Stewart when you really need her? But enough about my transient hotel troubles: I was now a New York City homeowner. After more than a year of renovating my dollhouse in the trees—an unfortunate plumbing accident triggered the flooding of every unit in my tier, and I think my insurance adjuster had to add an extra phone line to handle the screaming—I was finally ready to move into my diminutive (350 square feet) penthouse.

On a naive whim and to fit in with my new neighbors, I decided to run for a position on the building's co-op board. Unfortunately, though all looming water damage lawsuits had been amicably resolved, my history as the "guy who flooded the building" sunk my chances. Apparently, some people can hold a grudge even longer than they can hold a life preserver. In year two of my residency, I ran again and finally secured a coveted seat on the board. It felt like a real New York City accomplishment as I joined the ranks of my fellow disgruntled neighbors. "Damn those noisy tourists!" we'd decry. "Go back to where you came from and take your sticky Magnolia cupcakes with you!" Finally, I was almost a real New Yorker.

Barely a year later, I suddenly found myself unable to attend an important annual board meeting, the first time I had ever missed such an event. I emailed my regrets, informing all I wished to run again for my board position, hoping my seat would remain intact. I should probably rephrase that sentence, but in fact it's fairly accurate; my seat did not remain intact. By an overwhelming vote, my position had changed (see: title). I was now the president of my co-op association. *Oh shit.*

Rarely does a phrase evoke more moments of spontaneous condolence, often from strangers, than those confessional words. For anyone who has ever served on a co-op/condo or school board, there is an instant empathy for others in such a thankless position. Clearly the titles are given to those who glanced away for but a moment only to find their questionable skills have been hijacked by those who see a sucker born every other election cycle.

To date, I have learned that the best co-op board president should be equal parts Ben Bernanke, Judge Judy, Dr. Phil, and Xanax, preferably shaken, of course, not stirred to keep from bruising the disgruntled feelings of fellow members who are also trapped on the board. Say gin.

My co-op association often held their annual shareholders meeting in a lovely hall beside the chapel of St. Luke's in New York City's Greenwich Village, an idyllic setting, to be sure. Yet, if there was ever a patron saint of co-op presidents, I'm fairly certain Vatican II downgraded him to the remnant status of a reliquary. No doubt just a finger. You can guess which one.

As is my nervous want, I had been preparing for this particular meeting for months. However, as the weekend of the event approached, I grew apprehensive and even fearful. The yearly event was often filled with unhappy owners who used the forum to vent their loopy grievances. This was, after all, the evening's partial purpose. But keeping a meeting on topic often proved difficult when owners debated the merits of competing garden fertilizers or what could be done about those Airbnb marijuana parties.

Puzzling questions would fly, such as: Is an odor like loud music? Can a smell somehow be turned off at 11:00 p.m. on a weekday or 1:00 a.m. on a weekend? Can we at least agree the meeting must adjourn by 4:20 a.m.? Even the hazy wisdom of Cheech & Chong would have found these queries a buzzkill.

Earlier that day, I decided to take a break from my board meeting worries, noting a newly restored screening of Frank Capra's 1937 classic *Lost Horizon* at the nearby Film Forum Theatre. As a child in the late 1960s, I saw the film many times on television, replete with endlessly interruptive commercials for Frosted Flakes, Cocoa Krispies, and that stair-walking Slinky. It was a comfort film, transporting me back to my mom's house and the simple, long-ago world of a ten-year-old.

My mind hadn't changed much since those sugar-coated days: I still yearned to return to Shangri-la, the Himalayan utopia lost far beyond the cinematic horizon.

Set in the tumultuous 1930s, the film eerily echoes events of a futuristic twentieth century: a plane is hijacked and disappears amid the ominous clouds of war, the passengers unsure of their very survival. A worldwide search is undertaken, but the plane has inexplicably vanished, perhaps forever.

Though some seventy-eight years from spoiler alert, the characters have, in fact, been kidnapped but not for nefarious reasons. The high lama, who is hundreds of years old—don't ask!—watches over his flock like a loving shepherd. He has handpicked these chosen few to become his successors, most notably Ronald Colman, who plays a dashing foreign secretary, best-selling author, and lost traveler, along with several others, each for their particular skill. Now they've all been brought to Shangri-la to fulfill their souls and find their own destinies.

But as the film flickered and the images focused to my curious eye, the lilting voice of the high lama strangely began to resonate with me. Mesmerized, the words flashed before me as if written in a lightning strike, imprinting their brilliance on my clouded mind. "It is not an arduous task that I bequeath to you," says the high lama. "Preside in wisdom and grace while the storm rages. Be gentle and patient. Embrace courage to comfort and calm those you lead; they will be comforted and calmed. Then leading them to a better place will not just be an easier task; it won't be a task at all. It will just be."

It was, to be blunt, my light bulb moment without the screwing.

I realized then that my co-op, my apartment building, could be a utopia to its owners. It should be. It must. That was the goal, as impossible a thought as I could ever believe. Shangri-la was home. In that illuminating moment, I somehow knew I needed to find the courage to change: to change how I spoke to others, how I responded to issues, how I acted and reacted. I had to find an inner wisdom to set all storms aside. It wasn't the position of board president that was untenable. It was me.

Of course, like all great Frank Capra movies, *Lost Horizon* is chock-full of great truths. Perhaps I was most ready to hear this message as I questioned my own self-worth and validity. Perhaps only when you're the most vulnerable are you most likely to listen. Even to yourself.

Hours later, I found myself seated in front of the many owners and tenants of my co-op. I tried to relax, reflecting on the simple themes of the movie, and began to listen intently to every comment and complaint no matter how off topic the Q&A wandered.

I responded patiently, sometimes repeating the questioner's words back to them but without my usual snark and vitriol. I asked whether I understood their position correctly. Often, shocked at the calming edit, they nodded in contentment. Only then did I answer their questions with my newly discovered confidence, not arguing or avoiding but empathically embracing their issues. It took practice on my part, but I did it well.

Grace embraced.

"Yes, Agnes. Pot smoke, like loud music, can be very annoying. I'll speak to the tenant in unit 4G and see what I can do. I'm certain he was unaware of your asthma."

When an otherwise pleasant young man began to shout, I said: "I can't speak when you raise your voice, but if we both treat each other as gentlemen, the forum is yours. Please continue." His voice faltered as he repeated his complaint about the lack of hallway vacuuming in an easier tone. He found my comment disarming but not disagreeable.

Patience embraced.

Another owner suddenly and quite unexpectedly apologized for her behavior at past meetings. She acknowledged that the board's intention was to make things better for all and that she'd overreacted. Though still not pleased with the outcome of her grievance, she acquiesced to the board's decision and welcomed the improvements made to the building. "A better place called home," she added. She may not have seen the movie, but she most assuredly had her "come to Shangri-la" moment.

Wisdom embraced.

After the meeting, the board treasurer lingered outside, shaking hands with attendees and making small talk in the crisp evening air. He waved goodnight to an elderly owner as a middle-aged man ran up to him.

"I didn't miss the meeting, did I?" the man asked breathlessly.

"I'm afraid you did," said the treasurer. "We started at seven o'clock sharp."

The disappointed man stomped on the sidewalk. "Damn!" Then he suddenly looked up. "Say, haven't I seen you speak here before? Yes, you're very good. Very inspiring. So how did the meeting go?"

The treasurer waved off the compliment. "Good attendance. Some complaining, but overall, it went surprisingly well."

"Complaining? About what?" puzzled the man.

"Just the usual," said the treasurer. "Maintenance issues, rodent control, that sort of thing. But we're all good. In fact, most of us are going out for a drink now. Want to join us?"

The man gasped as the color drained from his face and he backed away. "A *drink*? What are you talking about? Isn't this the AA meeting?"

I hear about this curious incident hours later. Of course, we all had a good laugh, but I was also immediately reminded of the AA serenity prayer: *God, give us the grace to accept with serenity the things that cannot be changed, the courage to change the things that should be changed, and the wisdom to know the difference.*

Grace. Courage. Wisdom. Had the high lama—or more aptly, James Hilton, the author of *Lost Horizon*— once had a substance abuse problem? Was the high lama only high because he had so many pockets in his robe to stash a flask or a joint?

No matter. Still, the words reached out across the arc of time to me and resonated like cerebral fireworks on this special autumn night. Perhaps most prophetically, that prayer, attributed to theologian Reinhold Niebuhr, was written in 1937. Yes, 1937 once again. Hello, Dalai Lama.

In the days that followed, I receive many emails and comments from owners, most quite favorable. A disgruntled few remained, but now I corresponded in my newfound voice from my newfound self. The horizon's loss was my gain. All naivety aside, the old maxim still holds true: you can't please everybody. I'm certain even the high lama had a sheep or two bite him every now and then.

And that's why wool sweaters itch.

CHAPTER 11

FEE FI FAUX GREENWICH VILLAGE

A friend recently confessed to me his frustrating visit to the "other" Greenwich Village, the one located on the lower level of the New York-New York Hotel & Casino in Las Vegas, Nevada. He spat out an acerbic review that, at first hearing, seemed excessive. Evidently, the experience has crossed a very fine architectural line for him, most likely at the recreated intersection of Christopher and Gay Streets. He was angry and looking for someone to blame. "Block after block, it just goes on and on," he said bewilderedly. "All those fraudulent little buildings. My god, what were they thinking?" Then his voice dropped an octave. "And what's even weirder is that you're already there!" *Whatever that means.*

I had heard about the NY-NY's alternate reality and its bite-sized replicas of many an iconic Manhattan structure, but I was vague on the measurements, as well as the specifics. I knew a giant roller coaster somehow wove the disparate destinations together—just don't ask me how. The idea of a faux Greenwich Village was beyond bad taste bliss, but duplicating blocks of architectural history sounded as crazy as it might be wonderful. And who but a masochist or a kitsch addict would visit Las Vegas for the architecture?

Time to go whip shopping.

A few months later, I found myself checking into the Las Vegas Luxor Hotel & Casino, NY-NY's next "borough" neighbor. As nothing quite reflects fake better than a giant Nevada pyramid with Egyptian-revival furnishings that are beyond reviving, the stale decor seemed the perfect place to envy the dead.

I traversed many walkways, tunnels, and cavernously deep escalators within the bowels of the complex until I finally reached my destination. Like Oz on a distant horizon, the great false facade of Greenwich Village grew larger as I approached but not too large—just half scale, in fact. The fifty-plus faux vintage buildings formed streetscapes that retro-impersonate an area nearly half the size of an actual New York City block. I was shocked, if not amazed, but mostly a little nauseous.

Beyond the miniature canyons of eighteenth- and nineteenth-century structures, the townhouses and pubs, the apartment buildings and storefronts—some false, some real—the sense of village displacement quickly became apparent. Dreamlike, I walked down familiar streets that still were vaguely unfamiliar. In a haphazard fashion, it echoed the misdirection actual West Villagers feel, that off-kilter confusion of angled lanes just under 14th Street, the sideshow part of our Tilt-A-Whirl town. *I'm already there? Am I really? And where exactly is there?*

As I crossed yet another curious corner, the real became the surreal, and my friend's ominous words eerily turned true. Like a parallel life from the desert sand, before me rose the exact recreation of my own Greenwich Village apartment building. Though severely downsized, it still spookily replicated the place I now called home.

My jaw hit the cobblestones.

Over two thousand miles from my attic apartment at Bleecker and 11th Street, between a handicapped bathroom and a fake theatre facade, stood this mini doppelgänger. The details even mimicked the wrought-iron styling of my rusting balcony—the *only* balcony on Bleecker, as my realtor too often repeated.

The four-story structure was now barely two, yet the top floor was an architectural twin of my tiny penthouse apartment: an up-in-the-rafters studio that had once been a maid's quarters in this 1860s townhouse, then a painter's loft and that of an actress and a writer of soaps; most of them were crazy, or so I've been told. I still don't drink the water.

The effect, bizarre in itself, is less a creepy compliment to originality than a mirror of emptiness. This diminished perspective felt like a perpetual state of elsewhere, a smaller, if not unrequested, second serving. Or have I simply been watching too many *Pride of Place* episodes on PBS?

No matter the intent, Vegas's West Village was built to serve as amusement (see: feeding—of tourists). It's Greenwich Village as food court, not unlike the intersection of my real New York life as the noisy and over-sugared crowds outside Magnolia Bakery can attest—a place where only earplugs and clonazepam could permit a good night's sleep.

Though most of the buildings were architectural composites of countless other West Village structures, a long-time resident could occasionally spot an oddly familiar decorative element, filigree, or a corner where they were once mugged. After a time, this altered reality began to resemble the virtual world of a Hollywood backlot tour . . . just not in a good way.

Las Vegas's Greenwich Village attempted to convey a romanticized, historical society's gift shoppe version of yesteryear. Facades of antiques stores, a tailor, a barber, a milliner; they all added to the bland view of a sanitized, swept-clean version of the Village. Like post-Giuliani Times Square free of XXX-rated peeps, drag bars, tattoo parlors, questionable psychics, and a strictly enforced ban on eyebrow threading, it had been scrubbed clean of all character and characters.

Or, as an old-timer once wise cracked at the ever-changing face of Greenwich Village: "It's the end of an era . . . corn up my ass!"

Indeed.

Still, I was mesmerized. I stared at my own building for nearly an hour, waiting to see my "real" New York neighbors running back and forth in their circuitous routines: the actress dashing off to a callback, the realtor showing another closet-sized rental, those handsome college guys who seem to keep half the girls in the village satisfied. But alas, there's no in and out. I considered ringing my own bell but doubted I would answer. I pondered: *If imitation really is the sincerest form of flattery, am I just a mediocre version of me-lite?* Clearly what happens in Vegas didn't stay in Vegas, since it happened in New York City first and with better irony.

How many people could claim a diminutive, Disney-esque version of their home being open twenty-four hours a day? What were the odds of being reduced and replicated by a corporate gaming giant? And why do I smell of cupcakes once again?

It is difficult not to answer with a common Las Vegas sentiment: loss.

Startled back to reality as a siren blared across the casino floor to acknowledge a gambler's win, I looked about. Behind the real me was the fake me waiting for an *I Dream of Jeannie* slot machine to open up beside a woman chain-smoking English Ovals with her oxygen tank in tow. A bootlegged bite of the Big Apple was yet to be bitten. Not by me, at least. I was far from home.

Hauntingly, the food court storefronts echoed the same sad, mashed-up offerings of pizza, tacos, and one too many frozen-yogurt-dispensing kiosks to swallow. Just like on Bleecker, east of 7th Avenue. You know the block.

But the *real* Greenwich Village—the one of iconic history, the beat, the vibe, the essence, the spirited magic—could never exist here. Not even by half. Without flesh-and-blood New Yorkers bringing their chaotic lives into this odd homage, the point is moot.

In the end, it's simply a ghost town without ghosts. A small world after all and equally weird. Perhaps we could one day find someone to blame for this aberration, but I don't think he'd be home anytime soon.

My window shades were still closed, and closed they shall remain.

CHAPTER 12

THE
BEREAVED

I recognize many of you have other things you'd rather be doing tonight, so I'll make this quick. I myself have been binge watching *The Queen's Gambit,* and I cannot get those bouncing chess pieces off my frickin' bedroom ceiling at night. Goddamn Netflix, right?

With this stolen funeral home pen in hand, I've been scribbling down a number of things I'd like to say tonight and in no particular order other than the randomness of what annoys me about this particular wake . . . and the numbingly mindless comments made by the rest of you.

Okay, for starters: I did not know the deceased. I mean, at all. If I saw him lying in the street rather than in this rather inexpensive coffin, I'd have walked right by. Stepped right over him. To me, he's just another horizontal face in the crowd.

I'd venture to say I've never seen such a bad toupee, but that would be disrespectful to both the corpse and merkins most everywhere.

Again, I've never met this man; however, after hearing many of you tonight drone on endlessly with your exceedingly dull words of condolence—the dead wakefulness of it all—it's clear many of you didn't know him either.

Still, I'd like to thank the woman in black—and you know who you are—who blathered on for twenty minutes about her life, her loss, and the lack of adequate funeral home parking for her ten-year-old Subaru. To me, it confirmed the death of all humanity, but most particularly yours, madam. The only upside was that your coma-inducing eulogy gave me a chance to use the men's room twice and relieve myself of way too many easy foam lattes. Oh, and the "No Tipping" sign beside the bathroom attendant was also a nice touch, a great policy. I hate putting wet hands back into pockets, especially if they aren't my own.

As I was saying: I did not know the deceased, though a few of you somehow think you did. Maybe you came tonight to pay your respects or, just to be on the safe side, be certain he was actually dead. I saw a few of you poke him with hesitatingly curious fingers, so I figured that's what was up. I mean, if he owed you money, well, fuck—you're out of luck without a duck.

Now, when I first arrived at this funeral home tonight, I saw the roster of names listed in the lobby: Cohen, Saperstein, Neumann, McConnell. And that last name cracked me up. McConnell? I mean, who let him in?

But then I saw the name "Turtlebaum," and I knew I had to pop in and see what all the fuss was about. *Turtlebaum?* Now that's a funny name. What were his ancestors thinking? And why would turtles need such a salve? Sure, they're lying in the hot sun all day, but do they really need their own lotion? I half-pictured lubricated turtles splish-splashing about, and it made me laugh. Not that the deceased here looks like he ever cracked a smile, dead or alive.

Some of you may be thinking, *Why is this stranger standing at this podium eulogizing about a dead guy with a bad hairpiece and a funny last name? And someone he never met before, no less?* Fair question.

When I initially walked into the wake, I could see the crowd was a bit scant. Let's be honest: This is sadly attended. I've seen more people show up for a free STD screening at an IHOP . . . but I digress from the funereal fun.

Now, I'd like you all to consider the word "late." It's an odd word, most assuredly, but not in this situation. The dead guy here: He's not late. In fact, he was early; he's been here all afternoon waiting for all of you to straggle in with your HurryCanes and Hoveround scooters. This dead guy had his suit pressed, his face painted, and his clocked cleaned all while you people were still trying to think of a reason not to show up tonight.

Yes, I'm reminded of those stirring words from the Bible: Some are born late. Some achieve lateness. Some have lateness thrust upon them, like when they miss the bus . . . or go back for thirds at the all-you-can-eat Thai buffet. Those baby egg rolls will slow you down every fuckin' time. Now, I don't believe the Bible ever uses the word "fuck" but rather "begetting" or "begot." Seems a whole lot of "begetting" going on in Genesis— the chapter, not the band. And don't get me started on Two Corinthians walking into a leather bar . . .

Yes, yes, I hear your grumblings. I can see many tired old faces scowling back at me, some of them original, others badly reupholstered or seriously in need. I know most of you will be as horizontal as Mr. Stiffy here in a few short years, months, or perhaps later this week. On your way out tonight, some of you should check with the funeral director: he might have coupons. It's never too late to save a few bucks, and your kids will thank you.

I couldn't help but notice that not one of the previous bereavers tonight spoke of the deceased's religion. Maybe you knew him and thought he wouldn't want any prayers. Or maybe you just couldn't think up one yourself on the spot. Funeral speaking is not an easy gig, especially for those without improv training.

Speaking personally . . . sure, I could act, or more aptly, pretend to be the first man ever to go over Niagara Falls in a barrel or a young boy having his first erection. Or act as if I'm a docent at the White House giving tours, detailing historical points of interest about Warren G. Harding's colon. Heck, I could probably do all three of these things simultaneously: wearing a wood barrel, sporting a hard-on underneath, and still have the Second City skills in wielding some rather wicked gossip about the turbulent goings-on in any given Republican administration. I could do all these things, but would you really appreciate my efforts?

No. You've all got places to be banned from and people to disappoint. I get it.

Now, before I get to my ending comments on the finality of our dead friend here, I must critique that it would have been nice if there had at least been a glass of water up at the lectern for any oddly parched speaker. Or is that only offered in the deluxe package at this drive-through funeral home? Is it me, or is this wake very off-brand, very generic? It's as if they've run out of Ivermectin at Farm & Fleet and Aldi has introduced a discount casket aisle to compete with Costco.

Oh, just a reminder: I'm certain the family would want you to sign the guest registry on your way out; they're still speaking with people of interest concerning the murder . . . um, suicide. Apparently, "natural causes" is more akin to something like Green Peace . . . which, to my surprise, is not a website used to pick up cheap Irish girls.

And while you're in the lobby, be sure to snag the deceased's prayer card. I had no idea they still printed scratch 'n sniff stiff poetry. Smells like . . . heaven!

Finally, I think it only proper that we all take a moment and speculate on the type of person the decedent might have been in life . . .

For example: Perhaps he was a magnificent dancer . . . considering he was missing both of his little toes and a chromosome or two. A freak bowling accident caused the first; a genetic defect on his syphilitic father's side caused the second.

Or perhaps he had a badly descended testicle. Often, when turning his head to cough, the ceiling lights would inexplicably go out. He may have had one of the lowest electric bills in the state, but his penis cursed the darkness.

Or perhaps he was an expert in the pursuit of nothingness. If so, your grieving attendance here today would mean so much to him.

Actually, no, it wouldn't . . .

Though I'm not a religious person, I believe during functions such as this and others—weddings, divorce proceedings, IRS audits, the Hallmark Channel—a prayer is often welcomed. Unsure by whom, but we're winging it here.

I'd be remiss if I didn't at least say a few words to send this dead guy off, whoever he is or was—to wherever he's going or not.

Let us now bow our heads and watch our wallets and purses alike . . .

Life, my fellow bereavers, is like a milkshake for the lactose intolerant. You start out in a diaper, end up in a diaper, and shit away the middle of your life trying to figure the whole milk of it out. Am I right? Can I get an amen?

Oh, and who do I see about getting validated? Anyone? Not for my car, mind you, but for my existentially vapid earthbound existence.

CHAPTER 13

ESTATE SALES: AN ALIEN AUTOPSY

Over the last decade, the United States government has slowly been releasing unclassified UFO videos in an attempt to: (a) introduce the American public to the fact that extraterrestrials exist or (b) rack up millions of YouTube views for monetization to offset the national debt or (c) steal the high-altitude egos of billionaires Elon Musk, Richard Branson, and Jeff Bezos, the three space stooges.

As for actual aliens, we've now come to realize that for all their apparently advanced technologies, such as traveling at 13,000 mph, turning on an atmospheric dime, or avoiding the tumultuous TSA check-in lines at LaGuardia, the skills required to navigate a good—or, even more challenging, bad—estate sale seem to have eluded them.

I tell you this now as a basic fact, not science fiction. Humans, perhaps in spite of all our other flaws, are just better vintage shoppers. To that end, I offer the following conclusions.

1. LOCATING THE ESTATE SALE

Yes, the average UFO can spot a nuclear power plant from space, an Air Force base, or two drunks fishing in a boat at three in the morning. Big bang whoop! Try finding an estate sale where the street signs are missing or the estate sale company transposed the numerical address or posted the sale in the wrong town. East Dundee, West Dundee, unincorporated Dundee, Dundee without the "D," etc. *Please!*

Traveling at the speed of light doesn't get you to your destination any faster when the sale turns out to be in an adjacent coach house and not the actual advertised house. See, humans always get this . . . aliens, not so much.

I don't care how advanced their technology might be—no computer chip in their tiny gray heads is going to figure out that human beings can find an estate sale even when all the information they've been provided is incorrect. "Oh, is the sale *next* Thursday?"

Way before GPS, Siri, and your mother-in-law's misdirection materialized to confound your resale journey, serious vintage shoppers instinctively knew where any given sale was held.

I believe it's in our DNA that over the millennia, we as a species have developed a unique resale skill set to locate vintage merchandise like a truffle-sniffing pig. It's probably our only real skill. Well, that and complaining about the post office.

I've no doubt that some two million years ago, humans were climbing down a mountain to shop the cave sale of Homo erectus . . . and were damn excited to do so. Who wouldn't want first dibs on tetradactyl-sewn curtains? And don't tell me the cave paintings go with the cave.

2. STREET PARKING

Though it's impressive for aliens to cross multiple universes in the time it takes most of us to snag a cup of scalding coffee at the drive-thru window at McDonald's, the time saved really won't help our ETs at today's house sale. Dealers have arrived at the sale's location days, if not weeks, earlier. Human beings have been conceived, birthed, weened, and sent on their kindergarten way all while awaiting the start of a good sale. That said, all the best parking spots—especially those closest to the driveway—are long gone. Clearly, our alien friends have never searched for a parking spot at Costco over Labor Day weekend, a serious amateur alien move.

"Now, what's an ET to do?" you ask. Park their spacecraft in the neighbor's yard? Have they met Mrs. Kociscko, the inexplicably angry Polish woman who speaks no English yet has been in America for eighty-five years? Just a warning: she's got an antique broom that will make this alien probe seem like an atomic colonoscopy. Having spent a good portion of her life chasing drunken teenagers off her lawn, she'll be beating these little grays until they're black and blue.

Yes, our alien vintage shopping invasion is already off to a very bad start.

3. FORMING THE LINE

By this point in our lives, we've all seen those grainy videos of little aliens, usually in pairs or a set of three and usually in the forest, milling endlessly around their spaceship like incontinent members and looking, well, confused. Hey, it was a long trip, and I'm certain their tiny bladders can't hold much beyond a pass at any given Uranus.

Assuredly, they are all male aliens, as none of them would admit to needing a map to discover exactly how lost in space they've found themselves. One genital inch equals a billion miles, indeed.

Still, now comes perhaps their first big challenge: waiting in the estate sale line. I say "still" because this is exactly what they are *not* good at: standing still. And if there is anything dealers and estate sale aficionados will not tolerate, it's people (or whatever) who do not stay in line and/or are holding a place in line for someone/something else. Get a number, stay in line, and tell your frail friends to do the same. If they go wandering off, spinning over to the neighbor's lawn to take an alien dump, they're out. This line of vintage shoppers long ago decided: your gray/green ass—as in uneducated—is grass.

4. THE TAG SALE

Assuming ET and his big-headed buddies have made it past the front door—and that's a big assumption, given the competitive nature of those waiting in line—the resale party has only just begun. Now there's a mad dash to the bedrooms, the basement, the attic, and out the back door into the garage. Dealers and collectors are plundering the sale like a Viking orgy, snagging tags with little regard to limp limbs and southbound appendages. Shouts fly about the various rooms of the home, but the ETs are silent—vocalization is not their strong suit—and falling further into closets of resalable polyester.

Collectors rifle through stacks of vinyl while the ETs ponders what a Connie Francis might be, let alone be worth. Stacks of Pyrex fly past their confused heads like saucers in the sky. A large mixing bowl resembling their mother ship escapes their clawlike grip, but no matter; they'd neglected to notice the value-reducing hairline, and the aliens curse a silent sigh.

It is at this point that they mutually question why they'd attempted to crash-land into this sale to begin with. Initially, it seemed a good idea to bring back some earthling souvenirs—a kitschy keepsake after all their efforts impressing crop circles across the globe—separating wheat from the chaff has become unfathomingly boring. Plus, ten thousand circles later and these human beings still haven't decoded a single crop—so yes, they'd finally decided this particular Earth gig blows the big one, and it's time to shop.

Suddenly, everything is happening faster and more crushing than the last time they flew through a black hole . . . or Staten Island.

They may have the ability to levitate a Broyhill Sculptura dining set out the front door and into the yard, yet these ETs still don't have the skills necessary to navigate past a large-bearded man wearing a Divine T-shirt. Whatever a Divine is.

An old woman knees one of the ETs in the groin, abduction consequences be damned. And even though he/she has no genitals, the woman makes certain the ET doesn't reach the Eva Zeisel dinnerware. The alien

winces at both the pain created by this aggressive octogenarian and the loss of a scarce completer-piece ladle.
The gray-haired senior has seemingly outwitted an entire
advanced civilization of grays with a single arthritic knee
brace. *The Day the Earth Stood Still* was, apparently, just
another difficult Friday in late October in a far north-
ern suburb of Chicago.

5. THE CHECKOUT

Having spent thousands of years conquering hundreds
of worlds in galaxies innumerable, nothing has prepared
this ET and his cosmic comrades for what awaits. Marge,
the woman in charge of the sale, sits behind a table filled
with a laptop, assorted jewelry, price tags, a baker's dozen
of confections, and an industrial-size iced coffee from
Dunkin' Donuts. She is sugar buzzed, caffeine mean,
and not taking shit from anyone, human or otherwise.

Now, Marge has seen it all, sold it all, and has one
singular goal in mind: get this estate emptied, take the
money, pay the client, and get home to her five cats and
the mummified remains of her late husband in the basement freezer. To be fair, she only tells the above tale to
deter the cheapest of the cheapskate estate buyers when
they're fishing for a steal; it always seems to do the trick.

But back to the botched abduction . . .

Finally, and after much debate among the aliens,
the largest of the three somehow finds the courage to

bring an unpriced item to Marge's wobbly card table of commerce. Using only his advanced telepathy, he informs her of the missing tag, and she immediately shouts to all within earshot, "The Hans Wegner wall unit it *not* for sale, as I've told you people before. There was an NFS tag on it, and one of you ass monkeys took it off. I'm not announcing this again. Got it?"

The occupants of the room grumble back, with the bearded man emitting the lowest curse of the retro shoppers.

"I heard that!" Marge sharply echoes back.

But the big ET persists, mentally messaging Marge that they do not understand the problem. He concentrates on the words, *Why can't we purchase the floating horizontal design system of wood with hinged box compartment?*

"Listen, Extra-Small Testicle," she sighs in exasperation, "I don't know what your problem is. NFS means Not. For. Sale." She burps up a noxious cloud of pumpkin spice gas and spits out, "What else are you not buying today?"

One of the smaller grays puts a Holt Howard Pixieware mustard condiment jar on the table and attempts a creepy smile, resembling that of a difficult bowel movement.

Marge takes one look at the crazy ceramic jar and does a double take. "Friend of yours?" she says. "Cuz I never forget an ugly face."

VINTAGE CONFIDENTIAL

The ET leader thinks hard as he transmits his/her response, and once again Marge is quick to reply to the entire house: "No discounts on the first day of my sales!" Turning on him, she says, "The Holt Howard Pixieware jar is ten dollars, Phone Homeboy. This ain't a Leonard Nimoy film festival."

Now all the aliens begin to search their pockets for cash, which is difficult given they're not wearing any pants. Another gray thinks, *Check?* and Marge starts to turn a color brighter than the red planet itself.

"You gotta be kidding me. I'm not taking a check from you, and I'm being generous here, little people! You don't have ten bucks between the three of you? What's the currency of your planet? Cheese Whiz?"

One of the grays nods in Marge's direction and makes a cattle mutilation joke, now all of them having a bit of a silent laugh at the estate manager's expense.

Somehow, Marge knows she's been insulted, and she's done with close encounters of the cheapest of kind. "And no," she continues, cutting off the alien's thought, "unless Zelle is a princess from the star system, go fuck yourself. I'm not taking that or frickin' PayPal. Now get outta line. Don't you have an autopsy you're missing?"

The three ETs start to leave, empty-handed and ego bruised. The leader can't remember where he parked the spaceship on the crowded side street. They scan the neighborhood, as if searching for the eggs of a virgin, when the bearded man in the Divine T-shirt breathlessly catches them before they leave. "Hey, little bros. Um, got some bad news. I was turning my van around in the driveway, and I may have dented that weird Tylenol Airstream of yours. Sorry, but not to worry. I don't have insurance, but my brother-in-law is a body guy who can fix that hole right up."

The ETs turn to one another and grumble in triplicate space-signaling silence, "Oh, fuck me, fuck me, fuck me!"

CHAPTER 14

MISS SPOKEN

I am standing at the CVS pharmacy counter with my feisty eighty-six-year-old aunt. As is her style, she is dressed rather smartly in black slacks and a tailored blouse. Her hair is salon perfect, as always. It has taken her hours to be this beautifully presentable—all so we can pick up her numerous prescriptions and attempt to redeem the bulging fistful of coupons she now holds in her arthritic hand.

"Miss Baldwin!" says the handsome Asian pharmacist. "You look lovely this morning. How have you been feeling?"

The litany begins. Her back, you know, it's just terrible, terrible. Hard to move, hard to walk, the pain. Her stomach has been giving her troubles, has for years. And her bowels—she's usually constipated until she gets the "runs," and then it just doesn't stop. And the troubles "down there," well, it can't be mentioned but already has. And she has no appetite. And she's nauseous. And she's been so depressed, her nerves, you see, just terrible. Terrible.

"Oh my, oh my," he says, taking the prescription slips from her hand. "Let me see what we can do for you today."

"You know, I lost my sister six months ago—and my niece six months before that. It's been a terrible year, just terrible."

"Yes . . ." The pharmacist nods, having heard the stories before. His hands continue juggling an act of bottles, pills, and measuring scoops. "Terrible, Miss Baldwin," he consoles. "So terrible for you!"

My aunt half raises her walker toward the counter; it's one of those silly aluminum contraptions with two wobbly plastic wheels in the front and two worn rubber balls to the back.

"And *no* generics!" she shouts to the pharmacist, her hearing more functional than her aging self. "Like I've told you before!"

"No, Miss Baldwin. I know. I know. No generics. Give me fifteen minutes."

The pharmacist scampers off. I, however, am not so lucky. She shakes the coupons in her hand like a fan-flaming fire. "I need a lot of stuff today and this one

. . ." she grumbles, pointing in the pharmacist's direction, "he's slower than my shower drain."

My aunt is full of funny sayings, most of them original or at least original to me. In one of her classier comments—when finding some great mismarked bargain in the ladies' dress department at Marshall Fields, she exclaimed: "Well, hot snot and a barrel of puke!" Apparently, the phrase was quite the scandal in the 1930s, proving once again how timeless this lady truly is.

I once asked my aunt about her downstairs neighbor, a troubled young man who, from time to time, she would either take under her wing or mercilessly chastise. "You know, he's an inventor," she'd tell me with the straightest of face. "He's invented the world's first automatic ass wiper." While lighting a cigarette and exhaling, she adds, "And no one gives a shit!"

We zigzag through CVS, the walker scraping through the pharmacy like dull chalk on a broken board. I am convinced that in our wake, the words "HELP ME" are scratched into the linoleum floor. But a lad and alas, no one will be coming to my rescue today.

Raising her fistful of dollars yet to be saved, she laments, "You have to watch these people; they change the prices all the time. That's why I have these coupons."

To be fair, that's not the only reason she has coupons. Yes, she's thrifty, absolutely, but it goes well beyond that fact. Coupons are power, a sort of discounted influence that enables the holder to direct not merely a discount but a submission. It's rather the S&M of retail. Just ask any clerk. And my aunt can crack that coupon whip with the best of them.

Now we stop in a seemingly endless bowling alley–sized aisle of toothpaste heaven from end to hellish, squeezable end. My aunt begins the search for her particular brand—and size and price—like we're attending a Monty Hall memorial treasure hunt.

I grab various contenders, all with the same response: "No, no. That's the twelve-ounce; I want the eight-ounce." And: "Do I *look* like I need whitening?" And my favorite: "That'll dissolve dentures in a canary-mining minute." It makes no sense, but it's brilliant.

Her walker suddenly starts to veer her off in another misleading direction, almost as if it has a hazy global positioning senior mindset of its own. "I need Kleenex!" she complains. "The brand, not the tissue."

And this is how the next forty-five minutes progress. Slowly. Methodically. Maddeningly. Every aisle is over-choice, every selection is an over-selection, every decision an indecision, every potential purchase an opportunity for an impending swindle. Apparently, the store is one giant retail mousetrap, and we are coupon-laden mice sniffing out tiny tidbits of value in a world of questionably inedible cheese gone missing.

Many times, I try to take the coupons from my aunt's hand, somehow thinking she'll be better able to steer her walker, but she's having none of it. Either I'm not to be trusted or she thinks I'll stash half of those damn coupons into a deep coat pocket so we can finish our shopping before the store closes . . . or goes out of business. Honestly, she's not mistaken with either of my diabolically held scenarios.

To that fateful end: "No, no, you didn't have a coupon for that; no, I'm absolutely certain. You had one for the value pack, not the travel size."

I will most assuredly burn in hell later, but right now I'll be happy with a two-for-one on Bengay. Even if he's just bi-curious.

Over the intercom, the voice of an Asian god suddenly intercedes my coupon troubles: "Missy Baldwin. Your prescriptions are ready at the pharmacy."

Missy Baldwin, I laugh to myself. Perhaps I misheard, although it would be an audible foreshadowing of bad things to come.

My aunt pokes me with an insistent finger. "See? Slower than my shower drain . . . and about damn time."

Wildly wielding her walker, my aunt glacially shuffles back to the pharmacy as I wearily follow many steps behind. Rarely has moving this slowly been so tiring; such labored shopping sprees should be internet-broadcast sporting events of the future to be held in some parallel universe where space and time collide with broken shopping carts and empty containers of Metamucil, Excedrin, and Pepto-Bismol liquid, *not* the tablets. Such is the place where patience goes to die—because at least in death, there is an enviable winning.

Back at his window, the pharmacist hands my aunt her medications. She glances at them briefly then scoffs a scoff heard three aisles down, rattling the Depends display. She explodes with her trademarked vitriol that is usually only available as an aerosol fume. "I told you no generics!"

"Yes, Miss Baldwin," the pharmacist calmly replies, "I never give you generics." And here is where he makes his fatal mistake, saying, "Even though it's the same product for less money."

"It is *not* the same product. I cannot take generic medications. Are you trying to kill me?"

I smile to no one in particular. I can't help but notice a small group of older AARP-shy members slither from behind shelves packed high with Magnum condoms, off-brand lubricants, and a product called Calm. They've come for the ex-lax but will stay for the show.

"Miss Baldwin, I can assure you these are not generics."

Her four-legged walker now seems to levitate of its own volition—more likely powered by the four cups of coffee she drank earlier. Plus, she's been on killer anti-depressants since the 1960s. The good stuff.

My aunt is now at bat. The ball is pitched, and she swings: "Listen, Slanty!" comes both the home run and our final death-blow strike.

I'm cringing as she throws the prescriptions back at the pharmacist. The boxes hit him chest-high on his clean white smock, the vials falling to the counter like medicated confetti.

"I said no generics!"

The nearby octogenarian crowd seems to draw closer. Faintly, I can smell rubbing alcohol and old Vaseline. I'm almost certain that if reverse mortgages had an odor, I could have smelled them, as well, in that sickly second.

There is a short silence that only precludes those hesitating moments before something truly awful is about to happen. The pharmacist's once-comforting tone takes a discernable downturn. "What did you just call me?" he asks flatly.

"Listen," she starts, her tone noticeably lower, realizing she has gone too far.

Now I start to intentionally cough as loud as I can. My only dumb, dim-witted response is coughing in a misguided attempt to mask what's been said . . . as if my cough could turn back time and without any help from Cher.

"Did you just call me 'Slanty'?" quizzes the pharmacist. I roughly push my aunt and the walker aside, both making a squeaky shuffle sound as I attempt to intervene. But what quick fix could I possibly produce? Suddenly, I'm Monica Lewinsky's dry cleaner making excuses for the stain on that little blue dress. No Linda Tripp to tap. Plus, there's no coupon resolution to this big mess.

"My aunt misspoke, and I am so, so sorry. Truly." I start gathering up her prescription vials from the counter, but the pharmacist begins grabbing them back twice as fast with a crazed look on his face. And I can't blame him at all. But now every prescription vial has suddenly been pulled from the counter—prescriptions my aunt truly needs. How does one fix WTF?

"My aunt . . ." I continue, "she's depressed. I'm depressed. We've been through a lot this past year. She didn't mean what she said. Well, not like that, I mean. She's a sick old woman; she's unwell—I myself don't feel so hot right now. Listen, I am very, very sorry."

Now I'm waving cash around like I'm at the racetrack trying to bet on a dead horse. "I'll gladly pay for everything. Charge me retail. Generics are just fine!" I hear my own voice yet do not believe one word I am saying.

But the pharmacist just ignores me. He is done with Missy Baldwin and is missy pissed off. Worse yet, he's done with the both of us. And now he's on the telephone, speaking animatedly to someone.

Everything begins to blur. Years seem to fade away. I am now a little boy, maybe five or six, and my parents take me aside. I hear their repeatedly urgent words: "Be nice to your Aunt Bernice. She's sickly, always has been. She won't be with us long. It's only a matter of time. So just be nice—you be nice!"

Seventy years have passed. My aunt has outlived everyone in my family. The only person she hasn't buried is me.

And CVS is open until midnight. There's still time.

***

Belated Prologue

My aunt was born in 1918, the year of the Spanish flu. She, along with my mother and their siblings, were children of the Great Depression. "It wasn't so great," she'd often reminisce. "In fact, it sucked rotten eggs."

During those horrible years and into the 1930s, the family moved often, each place worse than the last—finally ending up in a church basement where they subsided on the handouts for poor parishioners. Often, they went to sleep—blankets on the floor, to be accurate—hungry. My grandmother took in laundry, mended clothes, washed floors, cooked, and cleaned.

She scavenged old rags and pots and pans, anything that could be turned into a nickel to feed her children.

At thirty-five, my grandmother died of food poisoning after traveling on an eastbound Chicago to NYC railroad run to locate a better place for them to move. Apparently, a silver-plated spoon was left to dissolve in an overly heated bowl of peaches, and botulism resulted. Within a month, my mother and aunt would be motherless; my mom was twelve, my aunt thirteen. Their mother's love was most assuredly the only love they ever knew and, possibly, would ever know.

My grandfather, once a wealthy builder, had lost everything in the crash of 1929 and became a brutally cruel alcoholic. He routinely beat his wife and children. I was told that my grandfather, coming home blind drunk one night and confusing the closet as a toilet— tried to rape my aunt while she was cleaning up his piss. His own daughter.

My mother was a handsome woman, stoic, and a serious survivor. But in her day, my aunt was the stunner; people often mistook her for Lucille Ball—she was that beautiful. After WWII, my aunt was nearly killed by a stranger, another drunk, in a random violent crime. He attacked her on the street, attempted to rape her, and left her naked and bleeding on the curb. Only the kindness of a neighbor saved her life that night. Years later, she was beaten and mugged in the vestibule of her apartment and, again, almost died from her injuries.

You see, this is the survivor I knew, and yes, respected, Missy Baldwin.

Does she have prejudices? Yes, as we all do. Not making excuses but rather acknowledging the troubling circumstances of her life. It's critical to remember she came from a different time and that her life experiences changed her as she lived and tried to survive whatever life threw at her. Which was much more than most.

We all take this journey to different destinations of resolve. I know she'd been horribly hurt by the men in her life and struggled to resolve the pain they'd inflicted both physically and mentally. Yes, she was a survivor, and those struggles created a troubling weight.

A few months before my mother passed, she made a big deal about needing to tell me something very important—something the whole family knew but had intentionally kept from me. The buildup held all the tension of a spoiler alert superstorm, but let me get to the punch, if not punch line:

"Your aunt," said my mother, as if divulging the location of Jimmy Hoffa's remains, "has been married many times."

"Yes," I said. "Three times. I know."

"No, no!" my mother corrected. "Four. She's been married four times. She married one man twice!"

Being the black sheep in the family—the "gay scandal," as my relatives would gossip—I found this to be hilarious! *Three marriages? Four marriages? Who cares?* Yet here was my dear mother, fighting for her life in the final months of cancer and wanting to release this burden by confessing her sister's additional marriage to me to "out" my aunt's truly mediocre secret.

"Like Elizabeth Taylor and Richard Burton . . ." I further defined.

"What?" replied my mother. "Well, yes and no. I mean, your aunt never got any decent jewelry from marrying that bum twice!"

***

I begin blurring back to reality. It is now three years after the death of my mother and sister, and I am completing my sixth year of family caregiver burnout as my aunt, so long ago destined for an early death, now stands stoically at the CVS pharmacy counter. Her thinning elbow is held in place by a large Black security guard.

In a fog, I glance to my side and also find my arm held in place by this same frustrated gentleman. He holds me tight, as if I might try to run away screaming to find solace among some sad Hallmark display. He grips me on one side, my aunt and her scraping aluminum walker held precariously on the other.

And yes, we are being escorted from the store like some elderly Bonnie and her homo nephew sidekick Clyde. My aunt turns, sniggers at the guard, nearly toppling over a tall stack of Brawny paper towels, and says, "Hey, I'm not done shopping here." She shakes the paper clippings in his face. "I still have coupons!"

"Sir?" I beg in a sad and final salvage attempt at pity. "Can she just make her purchases and we'll leave?"

The man says nothing. If only the same could be said of my aunt.

"Listen," she barks while waving an industrial-size bottle of discounted Windex. "I worked at Sears Roebuck for over forty years. Forty years! I like colored people. You can't work at Sears Roebuck and not like colored people."

Briskly, we are pushed through the store's electronic doors and out into the street like there's a sale on daylight. Together, we skid into our handicapped parking space. It happened so fast, sparks could have flown off the back end of that damn walker . . . and our sorry asses.

The security guard, now numb to whatever excuse my aunt may claim as defense, stands with his arms folded across his chest, blocking any possibility of our reentrance. "*Colored* people?" he shouts across the busy parking lot. "Oh, I can't wait to tell that to my friend Mr. Slanty!"

Aunt Bernice turns to me and sighs. "You better take me to another CVS. Some of these coupons expire tomorrow, and I've wasted more time here than I have spit!"

My aunt expired the following summer. I considered tucking coupons into her coffin but refrained.

Decidedly, Christ, the Ultimate Redeemer, must take it from here.

CHAPTER 15

CUPCAKE OVERDOSE: MAGNOLIA BAKERY AND ME

The *New York Times* real estate listing read: "An enchanting Swiss chalet penthouse studio. Imagine waking up to the sweet aroma of Magnolia Bakery . . ."

Oh, great, I thought. *A constant smell. Who wouldn't want that?*

The bakery meant little to me. As previously detailed, after spending three years trying to buy an apartment in Manhattan, I had all but given up. What I didn't purchase in the beginning of my search was now completely out of my financial reach. The year was 2005, and I had been outbid, outdone, and outwitted by the city's juggernaut real estate market. Could I possibly make one more run at the co-op windmill?

Did I ever think it might be nice to have an actual bakery across the street? Was I ever that young, that naive, that scent challenged? Yet Biography Bookstore was just two storefronts over from the apartment in question, which was a huge plus, and that alone made it a sweeter deal.

It was the middle of August. The apartment was a fourth-floor walk-up with a dead air conditioner the size of an Easy-Bake Oven that may have also been used for heat in the winter. This "penthouse" unit was up-in-the-rafters small. One dollhouse-sized wall comprised the kitchen with ancient cabinets barely hanging on, mostly half heading down and gravity bound. As I walked across the original oak floor, splinters stuck into the cuffs of my jeans like toothpicks on steroids. Built in 1860, poorly remodeled in 1960. And did I mention it was a few coins shy of $500,000? Other than those silly details, it was perfect.

And now for the clincher: The *New York Times* real estate listing finished with the words "Estate to be sold 'as is' within 48 hours. Best and final offer. A fast, clean deal." Or one could hope.

If the realtor hadn't liked me—I was on full schmooze—I wouldn't have stood a chance. Three offers for the apartment were on the table, and two bids were very close. The seller asked the realtor who wanted the apartment the most. And as he later related the story to me, he said, "Well, there's this crazy guy from Chicago . . ." and the rest was my personal victory.

Short story: I scored the property. Within days of the closing, I was perched four floors up and fifty yards away from what, I would soon learn, was one of the most famous culinary sweet tooth haunts in all of New York City. But I still didn't have a clue. My only view from the tiny top-floor attic window was the endless line of people standing outside of Magnolia Bakery. Every day from midafternoon to late in the evening, the faithful would arrive in prediabetic waves to pay their respects at $1.75 (back then) for a high-caloric cupcake blessing.

Our Lady of Lourdes may have stacks of obsolete crutches from answered prayers, but they were outnumbered by the thousands of empty Magnolia cupcake boxes littering the street and overflowing the garbage cans of Bleecker Playground, kitty-corner to the famous sugar fix. My appetite was quick to be neutered. "Never before has so much meant so little to so few . . ."

Was I the last person in the country to discover that Magnolia Bakery was a national obsession? When I told friends in other cities that I lived across from M. B., they knew my residence immediately; some knew my exact address and could even identify the building. They knew the doorway, the cobblestones on the corner, the particular smell of burnt sugar. Yes, of course, they also loved Marc Jacobs, Kate Spade, Biography Bookstore, Ralph Lauren, Cynthia Rowley, blah, blah, blah.

This seemed odd to me. It wasn't the infamous Dakota, the iconic 740 Park Ave., or the faux glitz pit of Trump Tower. It wasn't even architecture that put this vintage slice of the West Village on the map. It was those frickin' cupcakes.

In the business trades, Magnolia Bakery touted weekly sales of twenty thousand cupcakes plus untold other treats. Every weekend, thousands of people would descend on this quaint intersection of Bleecker and 11th Street: tour buses saddling up on the 9th Avenue side of Bleecker Playground, dispensing tourists like a pregnant guppy. In every kind of weather imaginable, the line extended from the door of the bakery in numbers seldom fewer than fifty and more typically over one hundred. And though the line moved smoothly, it remained intact for hours on end, like a favored ride at Disneyland. Or the King Tut tour of tooth decay.

"Famous for 15,000 calories . . ."

Magnolia Bakery began as a small neighborhood bakery in 1996 but has morphed into the stuff of legend: famous for being famous. It has been parodied on *Saturday Night Live* (6.8 million downloads, NBC claims) cementing its cult status like a clogged artery. A Magnolia cupcake with a single birthday candle made a cameo appearance in the film *The Devil Wears Prada,* just part of the story line, which coincidentally includes a $1,900 Marc Jacobs handbag, Magnolia's neighbor to the north. Of course, it was the thirty-second cameo in *Sex and the City* that helped turn the bakery into legend. By the time the *Sex and the City* movie franchise was released, those aging ingenues would be using buttercream as facials. Or wheelchair lubricant.

"Never forget your first time, unless it was totally forgettable . . ."

On my first visit to Magnolia Bakery, I made a massive cupcake *faux pas* by allowing two couples to cut ahead of me. Once inside, they promptly self-helped themselves to forty-eight cupcakes (Um, hello! The sign says: "Limit one dozen per person."), emptying all the trays in one swift swoop. For quite some time, no more cupcakes materialized from the back of the shop.

I must have looked disappointed. "Where are you from?" asked one of the husbands.

"Just moved here from Chicago," I forlornly responded.

"Oh, that explains it," he chuckled. "A New Yorker never would have let us cut in." He paused. "So what are you going to do now that we've taken all the cupcakes?"

"Well," I said slowly, "if we were in Chicago, I'd stuff your lifeless bodies into the trunk of your car and leave it at the airport. But since you're true New Yorkers, I'd use LaGuardia."

They promptly put two cupcakes back on the tray.

"It's like living across the street from Graceland . . . without the grace."
The crowds that amass in the West Village are a respectable lot. The daytime throngs are well-behaved, clean, and happy to be making the scene. Often people stand across the street, cell phones in hand, forwarding smartphone pics of Magnolia Bakery's Cracker Barrel–light exterior. There are often small traffic jams from the constant parade of town cars and Uber-Lyfts. The upside: you can always get a cab.

"This is the place I told you about," a girl shouts into a pink bejeweled phone shaped like Mickey Mouse's head. "This is where I am."

Not unpleasantly, the corner of Bleecker and 11th Street usually has a street carnival feel. On any given afternoon, an architectural walking tour maneuvers through the unloading of a bus of Italian tourists while a "major motion picture" is being shot down the street.

There are also movie location tours that make this a regular stop. Add to this the thousands of cupcake-starved patrons, and you have all of the ingredients for a sticky city gridlock.

"Night falls faster than dignity . . ."
When darkness descends on Fridays and Saturdays, a different kind of sweet decay comes out to prey. It's a younger Generation Y "Should I give a crap?" attitude, fresh from the bars, buzzed and hungry. Much like a West Village Side Story, there are cupcake scuffles: no frosting smeared but many an angry disagreement will arise among young men when they've been overserved, oversugared, and allowed to buy only a lame-ass dozen.

"Last call" at Magnolia has an odd desperation as the patrons roll out onto the sidewalk, laughing, cursing, and tossing empty cupcake boxes to the curb. But it's still hard to appear badass when you're sucking your fingers. If there's a potential "hookup" to be found, it's more likely to be with an insulin drip than a sexual assignation. But then again . . .

***

The following is a true story. I'm not telling it again.

It's 2:00 a.m. when a slick black town car pulls up to the now-darkened Magnolia. A young woman jumps out, clearly inebriated, and begins pounding on the bakery's door. "I'll give you twenty dollars for a cupcake," she yells.

Inside, a young maintenance man with a mop and bucket waives her off. "Come on! Twenty-five dollars then."

The man turns away.

She begins kicking at the door. "Okay, fifty. I'll give you fifty dollars for one cupcake!" More unintelligible screaming. "Well, how 'bout I fuck you for a cupcake!" And yes, she said *fuck*.

The worker scampers to the back of the store and turns off all the lights. The hungry woman returns to her limousine, sobbing. To the driver, she whines very loudly, "He won't even sell me one cupcake . . ."

"Life is not about frosting: it only masks what's underneath . . ."

The cupcake-crumb-eating pigeons in Bleecker Playground are fat and rush about like public school children on a vending-machine buzz. The nearby park takes a regular beating from the crowds and their confection wrappers; the nearby buildings routinely get ticketed for the trash that clutters the sidewalks, an unfair burden to the homeowners who try to keep this particular bedlam in order.

It's as if your next-door neighbor won the $100 million lotto . . . and you get to hose down his driveway. Not that M. B. doesn't try to keep its corner tidy. But even they could not have predicted what fame would bring to this tiny intersection of eighteenth-century streets and twenty-first-century baked goods.

Success, it seems, is one hungry, if not sticky, beast.

2022 update: Biography Bookstore was priced out of its old home and replaced by Bookmarc, Marc Jacobs's foray into reading. Of course, it's a hit. Lots of over-sized books with big pictures and ephemera kitsch; clearly, Jacobs knows his market. Jimmy Choo opened nearby and closed shortly thereafter with but a sneeze. Michael Kors and Ralph Lauren opened then closed as well. Coach and Burberry also both closed their double-wide stores. Still, Christofle silver has opened a dazzling little jewel box, and the street now boasts multiple perfume retailers. Upscale home goods stores and webbed-birthed pop-up retail concepts seem to be all the rage, for now. Bleecker Street has evolved into the most expensive game of musical retail chairs ever played. At its peak, the area has surpassed even the rental rates of Rodeo Drive. Go figure . . . and bring your calculator.

And Magnolia Bakery? Their signature Bleecker store is as crazy and busy as ever. They now have countless locations across the city and throughout the country.

"Can I fuck you for a cupcake?"

I think you already have.

Reprinted with kind permission, *Mr. Beller's Neighborhood/NYC.*

CHAPTER 16

DOWN-LOADING MRS. ASTOR

(Podcast Transcript)

Mrs. Astor (entering, she holds a laptop and whispers to someone offstage): Oh! Oh, my! Are you sure he's not here? Have you checked the basement of the theatre, dear? He's been found down there among the props before! No? Oh.

(To audience): Well, I'm afraid I have some dreadful news, just awful. It seems that Barry, the host of tonight's show has been . . . oh, how do I say this? Detained. I thought he'd be released by now, but the authorities seem to take a dim view of being overly affectionate with a traffic cone. Yes, it appears a simple parking ticket has now degenerated into an ugly morals charge. Clearly, the police today are using their overly endowed members to round up innocent cone-o-philes.

Oh, my poor Barry. This could have happened to anyone with a predilection for incident exposure during alternate leap years of Lent. I mean, what is this? Communist China or Florida at spring break? No, seriously, I'm asking; I have no idea where I am!

Now, I find this all to be very upsetting. Yes, Barry had the most amazing evening planned, an evening that would have been the change of life you've been looking for . . . without the hot flashes. You see, tonight—this very moment—is being broadcast live from a peapod! (Disoriented/confused) No, those aren't the right words. (Pause) Scammed! Yes, web scammed live across the internetta, a technological breakthrough of an infection. So many wonderful new ideas, so few effective placebos.

I myself am half-thrilled to embrace the future—so long as it wasn't inappropriately fondled yesterday-ish. Like so many of you, I also once thought the internetta was just another fine hair-care product from the makers of K-Y and Aqua Net. However, today I pay all my bills online, and I'm all about the socialists networking.

Oh, I'm such a twitter. How impolite I must seem to all of you who are barely paying attention. I've been meaning to talk to you about Alzheimer's, but I keep forgetting.

Now, my name is Mrs. Constance Astor—and though I possess a famously notable surname, I can assure you I am not related to anyone who went down on the Titanic or any other phallic-shaped vessel. No! I am a born-and-bred Chicago Astor. We do not believe in sea travel of any kind, lessening the chances of crabs, overly affectionate seamen, or berthing in inappropriate ports.

I realize that many of you tuned in—Is that the right phrase? No, that's wrong. Downloaded, that's it! (Pause. Mrs. Astor is corrected via an offstage voice)

What? Down low? No. No, that's not right at all. (Pause) What? That's not possible. Down low with Master Bear? What the hell is that? That cannot be the name of this show. Barry never said a word about . . . (Pause) Well, are you sure? I thought it was downloading . . .

We seem to have a difference of opinion about exactly what you're presently seeing. I believe this is commonly referred to a 'technical problem,' especially when it's someone else's fault. Now, this can happen at better off-off Broadway shows . . . often where uncomfortable seating is involved.

You see, Barry, who's my neighbor at Trump Tower Chicago, this was—well, is—his idea. He's such a dear boy, my Barry. Handsome, masculine, yet he so loves his antiques and decorative objects. I've never met a man so submissive to the arts. One day, he's modern; the next, mission—or missionary, as they say in the rough trade.

Why, just the other night, Barry was returning from San Francisco where he keeps an incontinent pied-à-terre packed with way too many Hummels. Strange as it may seem, he apparently had an unfortunate incident with a faulty metal detector at O'Hare—the airport, that is, not the Irish family down the hall that doesn't recycle properly.

Apparently, Barry had various internal objects unknown to the FAA or Homeland Security in his personhood. Now, I can't explain what happened—the X-rays aren't yet back yet from Walgreens—but Barry did call me from a poorly lit holding cell that he's presently redecorating. It was then he confessed to me the additional morals charge regarding a street traffic parking cone he named 'Desire.'

Oh, poor Barry. What's that old maxim? When it rains, it pours for whores? In any event—and I do apologize for this overly detailed, gossip-filled orgy of verbal depravity. I think this is covered quite thoroughly in the Playbill—but it was at this point in our conversation that Barry asked me to be the substitute host for the premiere of his new web show (slowly reading from a cue card): *Down Low with Master Bear.*

Now, are we sure that's still the name of the show? (Pause, waiting for the answer) Well, I'm just asking.

It seems inaccurate given that Barry is so rectally challenged. (Pause) Oh, I see.

I know what some of you are thinking: this barely
middle-aged woman—sure, she looks good for her
surprisingly young age, still has her figure, most of
her teeth, with men desirous of her in that 'urban
outsourcing' way—why would Barry want her to host
his show?

Well, it's all very simple, really. Everything you see
here has been prepaid. Yes, the theatre, the cameras,
that pushy director you hear babbling from offstage,
the adorable makeup boy in his extremely tight-fitting
pants. All done by Barry.

So I'm certain Barry's internally located paraphernal-
ia will one day pass. Everything does. All he needs is a
quick scat scan. But enough about the number two: How
about me, Mrs. Astor? Tonight's number one! Perhaps
it's time to go up my backstory . . .

(Clears throat) You see, I began my career as the
gardening editor for the *Hyde Park Herald*, Chicago's
oldest newspaper, founded in 1882. My column was
nationally syndicated for over fifteen years until an
unfortunate typo about the manhandling of pansies
and an ill-timed reference to the NRA ended my employ.

Of course, this all precipitated the passing of "Don't
ask, don't smell"—as if any of you needed another reason
to support Barack Obama. But you know what they say:

"Once you go Black, you can't take it back, especially without a receipt."

In any event: you've all heard of *Time Out Chicago* magazine? Well, I worked for *Time Served,* the bible of the federal prison system. Who's in, who's out, tips, snitches—the best way to clean a shiv—helpful *Helter Skelter* hints, that sort of thing. I wrote a personal advice column called Kisses, My Astor—as men in prison so often need to be lent an open ear, orifice, or helping hand.

And this is where destiny comes into play: it turns out Barry, my Barry, had a friend who read *Time Served.* What are the odds? I mean, why would Barry know anyone in prison? It's just silly. So, long story, short attention span. Ta-da, I'm here! And welcome to . . . Downloading Mrs. Astor.

(Offstage grumble is heard)

(Ignoring) Thank you for your less-than-enthusiastic applause. Now, before answering the many emailers and webbed scams from our heterosexually challenged viewers, I'd like to introduce my cohost and lesser half, Jackie Masonette.

(Mrs. Astor gestures to a chair; Jackie enters, sits)

Now, Jackie, I think that went very well, don't you? (Jackie barely whispers her response) Well, what about the title of the show, dear? (Pause) No, I did not change it—it's more of an update for accuracy. (Pause) Listen,

Barry called me from his prison remodel, not you. You don't know the first thing about overly intimate assignations on the internetta. As I recall, you once told me you thought a one-night stand was doing it in the dark vertically.

No, Barry and I have a special bondage, which is why he offered me his show. He even has a special pet name for me: Fagella-Hagella. Isn't that adorable? (Pause) It's a term of endearment. Whatever else could it possibly be?

(Frustrated) Please don't be that way, Jackie. Of course you're my best friend, but in a secondary fashion. You're like a sidekick. Or a kickstand. Or something you use to turn a lamp off. (Pause) No, not clap on. Barry specifically instructed me to steer clear of any STDs unless a 'U' was involved.

So, continuing: Barry will be contacting us tonight from time to time in a most fluid way . . . (Pause) What, Jackie? You don't like the sound of that either? It's a figure of speech, dear. (Pause) That's a vulgar thing to say about Barry's penile incarceration. Why, I cannot imagine the position he now finds himself in . . .

Now Jackie, why don't you tell everyone about yourself? (Pause) You're single, never married, and yes, I'm sure the listeners quickly figured that out. Yes, you are rather old, Jackie, but you could still meet someone at the senior center—or the elder hospice.

What? Well, it's true you used to be my maid, but that's ancient history. (Pause) I did not replace you: you were downsized extinct. And stop crying. Your life has not been a roller coaster of disappointment—it's more like Six Black Flags over Dismay.

Okay, now you're changing the topic. I legally adopted that child, Jackie. She needed a home that wasn't Korea. And stop saying 'that girl.' Her name is Park-All-Day-Fifty-Bucks. (Pause) She is not a slave! Cleaning seems to calm her nerves—especially the dry cleaning. So she enjoys clipping my toenails; one day she could become a world-class podiatrist. What better training than starting at the bottom of my bunions?

Now, Jackie—when Barry called me last night, do you know the first person I thought of? (Pause) No, not you, dear. Oprah. Her first show was *A.M. Chicago* . . . because it was broadcast in the a.m. . . . in Chicago . . . right after the sad local news and poorly predicted weather. A few years after that—*boom*—launches her own network. Now she's a billionaire . . . proving that even a dyslexic can spell oneself into a HARPO of success.

(Pause) Now, Jackie, please hand me our inaugural question. Thank you! Our first confused communiqué comes from Idaho. Oh, I just love Idaho. Have you ever been? It's truly the breadbasket of America even though it's just filled with potatoes.

(Reading) Dear Master Barry: Oh, sorry. Dear Mrs. Astor: I've recently come out to my family and friends, but it has not been a good experience. There are no bars here, and the only places I seem to meet men are at bookstores and truck stops. I'm an attractive twenty-year-old guy with a hot body and am very well . . . (Pause) I can't seem to make out this last word. Anyway: Why am I so lonely? Signed, Mr. Big in Idaho.

Um, Dear Mr. Big: I congratulate you on coming out, since you've obviously been somewhere else. Travel is always such a rejuvenating experience. Now you say you can't get any bars in your area? Have you tried another cell service provider? (Pause)

What, Jackie? Ga-ga-gay bars? Oh, the frivolity of drinking establishments. No, I'm sorry. No, no, I fear the drinking of assorted liquids from various taps will not bring you happiness. I mean: What satisfaction could ever come from simply swallowing? (Pause)

Oh my, Jackie. What's wrong, dear? It's as if all the blood has drained from what's left of your sagging face. I haven't seen such discoloration since Angela Lansbury hosted the Tony Awards. (Pause) Well, can you at least hand me the next disturbing correspondence?

Dear Mrs. Astor: Though born a man, I've recently had a sex change and am now a woman. However, I now find myself attracted to other women. Am I a lesbian? I want to act on these feelings, but I fear I may be missing something. Do you think it's my penis? Signed: Pro-Bono. (Pause)

My dear Pro-Bono, this may sound shocking to some, but lesbians do not have penises. Just ask Bruce Jenner. The last thing a lesbian wants to see is a penis—unless it's leaving the wood to make room for more beavers. (Pause) Now, Jackie—it's probably not a good idea to scream and vomit simultaneously. (Pause) What do you mean it's as if you've awoken from a nightmare only to find yourself inside another nightmare? Maybe you should stop binge watching *Squid Game*, given your seafood allergies. (Pause) Now, next question, please.

Dear Mrs. Astor: What's the difference between 'homo' and 'queer'?

Finally, an easy one: 'homo' is one . . . as in singular sensation. 'Queer' is Lacoste running out of alligators. (Pause) Oh, wait, there's a second part: transsexual and transvestite?

A bit more complicated, but I'll take a swing at it: transsexuals are seldom transvestites. They have little in common except for a mutual penchant for stylishly fitted footwear. From what I've been told by various inattentive Neiman Marcus salespeople, the lingo of today is 'trans,' as in transition to transgender and gears neutral.

Now, a transsexual may change seats in a restaurant many times, but eventually they'll order an entrée. A transvestite only wishes to appear that they've eaten.

(A chime is heard. Mrs. Astor opens her laptop and recognizes Barry.)

Hello? Hello, Barry? Can you see me? It's Mrs. Astor! Yes, I can see your face, too, dear, but that's all I can see. Aren't you a bit too close to the camera? It's like you're getting ready for a facial scrub. I didn't realize they had male technicians at Elizabeth Arden.

What? What, dear? What do you mean you're in a sling? Is that part of a special package? I don't understand. Did you break something? Your wrist? A fist? I'm confused. No, Barry, but you do seem to be overly excited for someone so horizontal.

Now, I'm happy to see you're out of prison, but just how did you find yourself so . . . ? Well, none of my beeswax. Yes, you're in a bit of a pickle. What? A jam? What? They're jamming what? A pickled jam? I don't think they carry that at Zabar's anymore, dear.

Well, of course I know what a gag is. (Laughs) I trust you're not pulling one over on me now . . . oh, a ball gag. No, I don't know what that is, dear.

(Pause) You're sounding muffled again, dear. You're being very unclear for someone with a master's degree in communication from the University of River Phoenix.

What's that? Well, of course I remember *When Tops Collide*. Wasn't that a science fiction film starring Raymond Massey? (Swooning) Oh, he was so reflective in his Teflon coating. (Pause)

Now Barry, it sounds as if you're in pain. I can't make out a thing you're saying. I don't suppose you can type with your nose? No, Barry, not your tongue. *Not* your tongue, dear! (Pause)

Oh, Barry, Barry, Barry. This must never be mentioned at the next Trump Tower Condominium Association meeting. I'm still making excuses for your inappropriate behavior with the ice sculpture at the Buddhist-Jewish-Muslim Christmas party. How many times must I tell you: Sterno cannot be sniffed near frozen holiday beverages. (Pause)

Okay. I'm getting your first instant message. How exciting! So many consonants and vowels: it's like *Wheel of Fortune* without that annoying Vanna White Castle. Okay, I see you're typing again: 'Send 4 more . . . men.'

(Concerned, pausing) Oh my, my. Now, Barry, far be it from me to intercourse myself into a situation, but aren't enough men already there? Well, it looks like the Battle of the Bulge without the costuming. I mean, this isn't a fraternity hazing, you know. (Beat) Oh, it *is*. I didn't realize. And here all this time I thought you were homeschooled. Well, of course, that would explain all those paddles.

(Pause) No, I'm sorry. Well, I thought it said 'men.' Oh, you're typing again: 'Send 4 more . . . meth.' (Confused) I'm so sorry, Barry. I really don't understand such diminished spelling. Can I buy a letter? Or perhaps a letterman since you've gone so collegiate? No? No more letters? Oh dear. (Pause) No, I don't understand. What's meth?

(Long pause) Don't get so angry. I had no idea of the pressures of fraternity living. Um, let's see. Meth. Method. Method acting. You're Lee Strasberg? No, sounds like meth. Breath? Death? Macbeth? You're holding auditions for *Macbeth*? Oh, I just love the classics. Perhaps there's a small part for me: I could be one of the more appealing witches.

(Mrs. Astor strikes a publicity pose)

(Frustrated) You seem to be getting angry again, dear. Well, just calm down. And you're so sweaty. Have that hairy frat boy with the jar of Miracle Whip towel you off. (Squinting into the screen) And do I see imported basil?

Oh, you're typing again: his name is Sergio. (Pause) My, you do have a stiff tongue. I've never seen so many salivated typestyles before—it's like: to hell with Helvetica!

Okay, here comes another one: Ba . . . bath. Oh yes. You certainly look like you could use a bath—you look like a slicked pig at a kosher BBQ. (Pause) Oh, wait, there's more. Bath salts? (Pause) Oh, I am a huge fan of the bath salts—why, it's the next best thing to a natural spring at Häagen and Dazs. (Pause)

Barry, you're shaking your head like you're having a seizure. It's obvious you require serious relaxation that doesn't involve lubricants branded Pennzoil. Now, I happen to know my dear friend Meryl Streep has a similar line of lubricants, but they're only available as a holographic gel.

Jackie, ring up Meryl and see if she has any gel left-over from her last cinematic reincarnation. (Pause) No, not from *The Iron Lady*. That would be Rust-Oleum. (Beat) No, I don't remember the name or fragrance. Holograms, dear, rarely smell like much of anything.

Now, Barry, I know it may appear you're having a lubri-cious barrel of fun over there, but as my late husband used to say: 'Someday your prince may come, but later you may find a small frog in your throat.' (Pause)

Hello? Hello, Barry? Barry? Are you there? Can you see me? Oh my, oh my . . .

(Shutting her laptop) Goddamn, internetta!

UPLOADING MASTER BARRY

(Podcast Transcript)

LOCATION: A MIDWEST FLEA MARKET, 1983

Father (to son): You see, boy, when your old man here was growin' up, I thought the future would be seein' TV on my wrist. That I could talk shit to somebody like on the phone but better, cuz it was like this two-way communication gizmo.

Hey, zip up your coat, Barry. These fleas are fuckin' cold in the morning.

Okay, so there was this guy, Dick Tracy. Well, he wasn't a real guy; he was more of a cartoon, but anyway he had the first one—this wrist TV phone gizmo. And everybody wanted one. Well, that and a flying car. Back then, they promised all kinds of shit like that to us when I was little, like you are now. But we got nothin'. They

177

promised us everything, but we got shit. The future—fuck, all of America turned into promises-o-shit!

(To customer) Hey! Hey, lady! Ya wanna see the first mobile phone ever? Got one right here. It's a phone ya can take anywhere. (Pause) No, ya don't need no cord from your house! Ya know how fuckin' long a cord ya'd need? Ya outta your fuckin' mind? (Pause) Hey! Hey, lady, come back here and check out this goddamn phone. Come back here, ya stupid bitch. (Pause)

See, Barry—these people, they're stupid. They can't see this is the future. But I can see the future, boy. It'll be this phone. First time I saw it, I knew it'd be big—frickin' huge. Well, yeah, they are kind big and heavy, but they aren't for fairies, ya know? Which is why I took this stall out here at the flea market. Ya gotta sell stuff to people—stuff that they don't even know they need yet. 'At's the secret of life, my boy.

(To customer) Hey! Hey, Julio! Hey, long time no-whatever-that-means, right? Hey, how ya been? So let me ask if ya ever see one of these cellular phones before? Well, let me show it to ya. Comes in this luggage case you carry over your shoulder. No, it ain't a purse! Ya think I'm out here at the flea market selling purses like some fruit? I'm selling tomorrow here. If your head wasn't so far up your own ass, you could see that, ya stupid motherfucker. Yeah, whatever. Go fuck yourself, you fucked-up fuck! (Pause)

Don't waste your time with losers like these, Barry. You gotta make somethin' of yourself. And stop with all this sissy stuff; no more buyin' disco records out here at the flea. You're embarrassing me. Ya gotta straighten up, boy. Be your own man. Be the top dog. Don't let nobody hold you down. You do this . . . and you'll have everything, especially all the pretty ladies. Now watch what I do . . .

(To customer) Hey, *mamacita, mamacita!* Ya ever see a cell phone before? Yeah, yeah, I know it kinda looks like a purse, but inside is this phone you can use anywhere, see? Look, it ain't heavy. You look strong. How many kids popped outta you? Whaddaya mean, 'That's personal'? You look like you banged out quite a few. Now come see this phone I be sellin' . . . hey! Hey, so what'd I say, what'd I say? Fuckin' *puta!* (Pause)

See Barry, that's called salesmanship. Good for you to see what your old man does for a living. Your mother, she thinks I'm crazy. But I'll tell you a secret: I got her to loan me the money to buy these phones to resell in the first place. So, like, who's the crazy one now, right?

(To customer) Hey, chief! How ya doin'? You ever see a mobile phone before? No, it's not a brick! Ya think I'm out here in the cold-sellin' bricks? It's a frickin' cellular phone, the latest thing. Whaddaya mean, 'What does it do?' With this thing, I can call your mama from right here and tell her to suck my . . . Hey, you come back here, ya lousy piece a shit! (Pause)

See, Barry, ya gotta do something with your life. Be somebody. Hey, I could be banging a dozen bitches a week, but I got these mobile cell phones to sell. Hey, wait! That's fuckin' funny; cell phones to sell.

(Loudly to anyone) Uh, sellin' cell phones here! Get your cell phones . . . 'fore I sell out. Sellin' cell phones here! Cell, cell, cell . . . sold! (Pause)

Ya gotta put yourself out there, Barry. Gotta be smart. Gotta reinvent your future 'fore it gets messed up like mine. It's the ABCs: Always Be Cruising—for sales.

(To customer) Hey, pretty boy! Yeah, you with the scarf, come over here. You ever see a mobile cell phone before? Your *papi's* got one, even better, boy! So why not you? No, you *can* afford it. But I gotta say, you awful dressed up for a guy who ain't a lady, you don't mind me sayin'. . . not that I mean you're a fruit, unless you is . . . cuz you kinda look like a homo in that scarf and all. Anybody else ever tell you that? Yeah, well, maybe never mind. (Pause) Okay, so let's start over: This phone comes with a plan, see... five hundred free minutes. Maybe you call all your homo friends, right? (Pause) Plus it comes with this beautiful . . . um, purse! One hundred percent real black vinyl. (Pause) How much is it? Um, normally eight hundred dollars . . . but since you don't look so normal, how 'bout seven? Too much? Well, we can figure something out.

(Pause) Say, have you met my son, Barry?

LOCATION: TRUMP TOWER CHICAGO, 2015

Mrs. Astor: (slowly) Hello, Barry? It's Mrs. Astor? Yes, I'm Skyping you, dear. Is that the right word? Skyping? I have no idea what I'm doing, but yes, I'm Skyping on the internetta!

Am I calling at a bad time? Looks like you're hosting a party, but Barry, you promised me no more parties. (Pause) Now, Barry, I'm sorry, but this won't take but a minute. You did such wonderful work redecorating my apartment that it's being featured in the *Huffington Post*. At first, I thought it was a publication devoted to breathing issues, but apparently, it's a well-regarded online left-leaning screed. Yes, a shame about that, but still— you're now a nationally recognized interior designer, dear . . . very much in demand, to be sure . . . and not just by all those boys presently around you.

To think you started at that horrible flea market with your father. Oh, I remember him well from my days working at the prison . . . even the cockroaches didn't like him—and they liked everyone. Anyway, are you sure I'm not calling at a bad time? I'm thinking of having you remodel my guest bathroom, not that I ever have any guests. What do you think of a steam shower? (Pause) No, not a steam room, dear. A steam *shower.* You seem rather distracted, Barry. Can you tell that man behind you wearing the Guy Fawkes mask that you're on a significant telephone call with a client of import and tastefulness? (Pause) You have a taste for *what*, dear? Crocs? I hardly think now is a time to be discussing casual footwear while my bidet is up in the air.

Now, Barry: What about my steam shower? Do you think you could start next week? If possible, I'd like it finished before Ramadan . . . for personal reasons. You're shaking your head *no* again. To the steam shower or my religious timetable?

And can you have someone else hold your cell phone, dear? From all the shaking and vibrations, I feel an episode of vertigo coming on . . . and you know how I detest those silly Hitchcockian ingenues. (Pause)

Hello? Hello, Barry? Are you there? Can you see me? It's Mrs. Astor! Ugh! Goddamn internetta!

LOCATION: CHICAGO, PRESENT DAY

So my old man died last week. Christ, I hadn't thought of him in years. Of course, I was dead to him anyway—his son, the famous fag interior designer—a most successful sissy. I think it was all too much for him.

Yeah, what would he say? Oh, yes: 'America is promises-o-shit.' And for him, he was right. He was right about the phone, too, the crazy fool. And the future. Damn if it wouldn't be all about these frickin' cell phones.

Too bad his timing sucked. But it was so much more than the phones with him; he couldn't get out of his own damn way. Sometimes in life, you just can't get over yourself.

So, yeah, I got stuck with a garage full of those gigantic brick mobile cell phone bastards. Ended up donating the bunch. Who knew they'd be worth a small fortune now? And hell, if those carrying cases were any bigger, I could've buried him in one.

Still, thinking back on those long days at the flea market—God, how I hated them. Getting up in the middle of the night, pitch black outside, setting up those folding tables in the cold. And then, so damn slowly, the day would go from cold to hot and even hotter . . . until I'd burn my hands on everything I touched. From frozen to burnt, that was the routine of every damn weekend.

True story: I once saw an iguana at the urinal in the men's room and almost pissed myself. A filthy place that always smelled of pee. No doors on the stalls and the room filled with ancient old guys of every cruising creep.

But there was this one time when I couldn't have been more than sixteen. I thought I'd caught the bright eye of this sailor, most likely from the nearby Great Lakes Naval Base. He didn't look right at me but kind of turned while he was pissing, glancing aside like he was having the piss of a lifetime. You know when you need to go so bad and you finally do, so it's like the best moment of your entire life? Well, that was the look on his face. Fucking. Total. Bliss.

I remember the cold of his blue eyes flashed right past me. It was just for a second, and nothin' even happened. It was, like I said, ages ago, but I can still see those crisp white pants, that stunning face, the swipe of his big black 'stache, and hair tousled from the air of seas I'd never see.

You know, by now I've cruised a thousand dudes. But I'll never forget that singularly sexy face. He looked at me for a breathless second like he was holding a lucky lotto ticket—which I guess he sort of was, if you know what I mean. Eh, fuck a duck. No luck for this flea market boy. That sailor zipped it up and dashed back to some dizzy arcade girl, no doubt. Hope you gave it to her good, Mr. Sailor Bliss.

It's funny how life can turn on the sliver of a time. Funny how I didn't look for him then—haven't stopped looking for him since.

I remember hearing my father screaming as I lingered too long at the men's room mirror, combing my hair over and over, as if waiting to groom a groom that would never be.

But, hey. You know the only person to show up at my old man's funeral? Mrs. Astor. She's a nut, that old broad. Crazy as kittens at Christmas! And you know what else? She gets me. She's the only one . . . who ever really got me.

At the wake, she reminded me that she had Skyped me at an orgy. Man, I do not remember that at all; I must have been totally wasted. She was cool about it, though, and even gave me some "holographic gel," whatever that is. Told me to write a thank-you note to frickin' Meryl Streep.

Or as Mrs. Astor once quipped, referring to herself, Meryl, and me: 'The three of us make quite a pair!'

CHAPTER 18

THE DEPRESSION BAR

How many therapists does it take to change a light bulb? Only one, but first the light bulb has to really want to change.

Two weeks after I wrote that joke, I tell it to my own therapist. Two weeks after that, he drops me.

Now, I've been dumped by family, friends, lovers, my barista—but by my own mental health clinician? This is a new low, even by my ever-depressing standards.

Initially, my therapist offers a limping excuse about needing to finish a book he'd been writing— or reading.

Then again, I seem to recall him once telling me he'd received a grant to finish his research, which was either about securing grants or Ulysses S. and his mother. Apparently, they had issues.

I tell myself that perhaps he needs time to clean his office carpeting; traffic patterns from the depressed can severely wear on synthetic poly blends—sadness being the toughest stain to remove after stigmatic blood splatter. Just ask Vatican housekeeping.

Or maybe he has an embarrassing infestation of schizophrenia—that he has sprayed and sprayed yet still no luck in fumigating multiple personalities who've smelled amuck. Nothing worse than group BO.

I tell myself lots of things, often and to no avail. Still, somehow it seems equally sad that electroshock therapy—like haberdasheries and lobotomies—have gone so quickly out of fashion. All I have left is the hat on my head.

It is impossible to ignore the middling madness I am feeling in these seven stages of classic grief: shock and denial, pain and guilt, depression, an upward turn, reconciliation, acceptance, and hope.

Now I am stuck somewhere between an "upward turn" and having my parking ticket validated by a less than cooperative app. To me, it feels more like I've been upstaged in grief than staged like some badly furnished apartment rental.

The rejection sinks slowly into my stubborn head. "You're closing your practice? You're letting all your patients go?" I mumble in disbelief.

"Not exactly," he says sheepishly. "I'm keeping half a dozen patients. Maybe ten."

Ready. Set. Ouch. I feel like a swatted fly, momentarily stunned; I'm not dead yet, just buzzing in a confused numbness.

I slowly dip my toe into the cold news. "So, how did you decide who stays and who goes? I mean, why didn't I make the crazy cut? How did I miss that deep depression bar?"

"It's not like that at all!" he says in a fluster. "And there was never a depression bar." His words seem dryly dramshop.

"Then, why is it," I delicately ask, "that I have success down to a science and failure down to an art?"

"No, no!" he insists. "You perceive failure as a lack of success. It's by failing that you find success. In fact, it might be what you do best. Have you ever thought of that?"

There is an awkward pause and a mutual flinch between the both of us. Finally, he coughs up the explanatory words: "What I mean is . . . very few people can turn tragedy around faster than you. Your resilience may be your finest asset, your best success. Maybe that's the highest high."

I pull back from that revelatory headline. "Wow!" I slow gasp. "This rather feels like some Agatha Christie mystery solved in the final act: 'Curtain Calls the Drapes!'"

"Oh, I like that!" he purrs. "It's so . . . fitting!"

Apparently, I wear my sadness on my sleeve, and a short sleeve at that. "I could use a drink at that depression bar about now," I lament.

"There is no depression bar!" he snaps back, clearly annoyed with the phrase. "You really need to let go of that imagery."

Now, my comments just aggravate him—yet another gift of mine you can't return.

"Yet here I am!" I whine. "It's like I'm losing my favorite bartender."

"Now that's funny," he says without a smile. "You always make me laugh. And cry. I am going to miss you."

"I'm going to miss you too."

I truly mean those words. I've traveled many difficult years with this man, and he has been a vital link to my coming to terms with what has happened in my life. I have no way to measure the personal, tension-filled toll expended in seven-plus years as a family caregiver, living through the loss of life after life after life.

It feels, to be bone-cutting honest, that if there is provable life after death, there just isn't a life left for me.

"I'm sorry I'm so slow to reject," I say in a seemingly unresponsive yet verbalized trance. "I should be going, then?"

He nods.

I pause to take in the longest moment I can recall in my living memory. Longer than watching family members pass. Longer than multiple last breaths in hospitals and hospices. A long, time-suspending pause that defies acceptance of what lies lifelessly before you.

Thinking out loud, my realization announces: "I've never been dumped by a therapist before."

"Don't think of this as a *going* . . ." he reminds me, handing me my hat. "It's more of a . . . going *on*."

"Interesting." I swallow. "I just thought I'd know when it was time to go. By me, I guess. Who knew it would be today? Other than you, I mean."

"See!" he shyly beams, his hollowness a faux sincerity. "That's why I think you're ready."

I move to the door to leave then stop short. It all rumbles inside me now, and I find myself spitting out words I'd never before had the breath, or perhaps courage, to say. "You know, what's ironic here—I mean about my not making the crazy cut—is that I came to you about issues of loss. Specifically . . . endings. And now you and I are ending so abruptly. I mean, I guess this had to end eventually, of course, but so soon, so suddenly. Yes, this very much feels like another death. And not yours, my friend."

I return my hat to my head. "Mine."

His face droops to a sad pout. All is moot. He is mute. My therapist is really letting me go.

The finality floods through me in tears shed both long ago and yesterday. My father died in 1993. My boyfriend died that next year . . . at twenty-eight. My treasured sister followed at age fifty. My mother died six months later.

My only remaining relative, a maddening aunt who I so loved, became my emotional ruin. Her difficult final years and subsequent death was the burned-out caregiver's final scorching straw. Not her fault, yet not mine. Her passing ultimately stops this long, multiple-song cycle of death, sending me to this therapist couch, chair, and often, floor.

Now everyone is gone once again. Every. Last. One. Endings back to back to back.

I step into the hallway, holding tight to the doorknob for balance, for confidence, for what-the-fuck sake. I take a last look at my now "ex-therapist."

"How many therapists does it take to change a light bulb?" I ask with the glimmer of a newly found me.

"One?" he guesses or perhaps remembers.

"No," I correct. "Half a dozen. Maybe ten. But first the light bulb still has to really want to change."

CHAPTER 19

A SOMEDAY DREAM

What heights of joy bless each success—What depths of blame haunt every failure.

—ANONYMOUS

1985: Genesis

Evelyn and George had a plan. Smart, seasoned, headstrong, and perhaps a tad overconfident to their mutual faults, each knew what they wanted and intended to follow their plan as envisioned. The idea was familiar, but the location of their endeavor would be curious, if not noble. Best intentions aside, the two had a single creed: support an economically depressed, long-dismissed neighborhood and launch their vintage brainchild.

Individually, the skills of George and Evelyn might have found limited success; however, together their joint skill sets could drive an old-fashioned idea in a very new way. Evelyn brought the vintage element—her power thrift shopping made her a near legend in Chicago; her siblings tagged her with the nickname slur "Pickaninny" as both a pun and a compliment to her considerable "picking" skills. As politically incorrect as the term was, Evelyn made it her own and ran with it. "Cultural appropriation, my fine ass!" Evelyn cooed. In a single word, the racial race went to the swift, if not the swiftest.

George, her "lesser half," as he joked, knew little about retail or resale. His passion was real estate, and he'd been fascinated with every aspect of it since he was a small child. His grandfather owned his own home decades before most Black men of his generation. George's father followed that lead and, eventually, purchased a sprawling six flat near 57th Street and South Lake Shore Drive in Chicago. Even though the lake views could barely be seen from many blocks away, the apartments themselves were huge eight- to twelve-room affairs, most with four or five bedrooms, two or three bathrooms, and a tiny servant's room and bath.

George's parents raised their big family in one of those third-floor walk-up units: five kids, two aunts, an uncle, and Dora, the housekeeper/nanny/peacekeeper, making eleven people in all. Yet it was Dora who raised George, more or less—the less when he paid no mind to anyone or thing; the more when he listened to Dora's life lessons and attempted to step into the long shadow of his father's success.

It's within this backstory that George began his own life and made a series of real estate and business ventures that ranged from badly timed to inevitably unfortunate. In between, he made a few bucks from random, smaller deals gone green, but the lion's share of his financial roar was more often a sad meow. He had the passion of his father and grandfather but rarely the luck.

And then he met Evelyn. A cousin ragged him about attending a church BBQ on a random Sunday afternoon. He'd rarely gone to any church service— bribed with a post-sermon rib fest or otherwise—it just wasn't his thing. But on this particular Sunday, well, BBQ sounded like it would hit the spot. So he just skipped the service and showed up for the ribs and piles of potato salad.

George sat alone at a picnic table in the church's parking lot when a beautiful plus-size gal sat beside him and asked, "There room here?" She spread out her plate and soda before he had a chance to answer. He'd barely swallowed when she asked him something about the jacket he was wearing. His only thought was: *Huh?*

"It's, um, plaid," George said before pulling the last of the tangy rib meat off his latest bone.

"It's buffalo plaid," purred Evelyn. "Fits you well. Very smart."

George grabbed for a handful of paper napkins and wiped his mouth, heavy with sauce, and his lips in search of a saucy reply. He prayed the lump in his throat was not a rib bone and fretted a response. *Swallow, swipe, sweat, repeat.* His mind was blank. He had nothing.

Quickly recognizing her comment had caused a curious reaction, she grabbed the edge of George's coat sleeve, nearly snagging a loose button. "I mean," she continued as poor George barely caught a breath through the pause of her paws. "I meant, it's a sexy look." George's face remained frozen. "You see," Evelyn demurred. "I sell vintage clothes—you know, old retro clothes. And that's a *great* jacket. People want jackets like that. Very salable."

George bristled at her implication. "Hey, I'm not poor, lady. I don't have to sell my clothes to eat."

"Oh, I didn't mean . . ." Evelyn's words tripped from her own lips without finishing the thought she hadn't fully conceived or completed.

The next ten minutes would prove to be the quietest of the afternoon, with George perplexed by the intent of his picnic table companion and Evelyn rethinking her comment as an unintended insult. Finally, after yet another uncomfortable five minutes of silence that metastasized into a stagnated twenty, Evelyn turned to George. "So how's the BBQ?"

"It's good. I'm glad I came."

She smiled. "And what did you get out of pastor's sermon? He was certainly under the Lord's powerful good graces this morning!"

George was beginning to have serious mixed feelings about this woman, first thinking he was poor and—worse yet—now asking about a sermon he hadn't shown up to hear. Attractive—no, very sexy—but he didn't need to be rescued by any woman. Still, he knew fire when he saw it and liked the smell of smoke.

"I thought," George said, trampling into a lie, "the pastor missed a chance to preach about the poor. He said good words but not enough about the poor."

Evelyn's mind lit up in laughter, but no smile came to her face. "But the sermon's topic was the piousness of poverty."

A growing smirk passed across George's face. "Well, yeah," he chuckled, "but it's not like the poor have a monopoly on being poor. He could have told some famous Bible story to make his point better."

Pause, maybe five seconds tops. Evelyn and George simultaneously burst into laughter like a deleted outtake from some ancient William D. Foster silent slapstick. Evelyn saw George's bullshit answer as hilarious, and George saw a woman he needed to kiss. Like right now.

***

1987: Location. Location. Location.

George and Evelyn would date, mate, and marry—in that order—and move forward in the creation of their new baby: a vintage store. Month after month, the two canvassed the far South Side, west side, and any inner-city neighborhoods that might need an injection of retail with their bold idea; there were so many neighborhoods to consider. George delivered countless real estate listings to Evelyn, all contenders without winner. None would ever match the place Evelyn envisioned in her mind.

Together, they decided to search for a rather odd hybrid of a neighborhood, an area that would best suit their idea to make this concept work. An area not on the upswing but perhaps an old retail district where people had stopped shopping decades earlier. To others, this might seem a peculiar choice, yet this location was chosen to better both their own resale plans and the neighborhood they would eventually serve.

Finally, after nearly driving their troublesome van into an early auto graveyard, they stumbled on an old wooden A-frame structure in Hegewisch, a distant South Side neighborhood of Chicago. "Five more minutes of driving east and folks would be calling us Hoosiers!" lamented George. Still, he was happy to keep Evelyn happy.

Stuck in the middle of a lackluster commercial block of mostly empty storefronts was their new resale/retail baby: a beat-up, boarded-up, and apparently abandoned building. It was a deep lot and more space than they could use: a two-thousand-square-foot first-floor store with a full basement and two equally large apartments above. The old building was capped by a huge attic within the top of the structure.

A Vintage Thrift: Buy and Sell, the name of their new endeavor, would be born here. A "buy" shop, meaning a place where neighbors could bring their items to be sold—and "sell" being their resale destination. Evelyn wasn't fond of the consignment game: too much paperwork. Besides, she'd rather control both ends of any transaction. *This idea was a winner.*

In the fall of the year, George and Evelyn moved into both of the notably run-down apartments; George took the back unit and Evelyn the front, where it was a tad warmer with a few rattling radiators. The remodel consisted of painting—they had little money—and their new store would receive the same treatment, often with the same upstairs colors.

Evelyn, for her part, went shopping. She had found her place in the universe—and it was this location, location, location of this little building on this particular block of stores. There were no fewer than four other resale stores within a few hundred feet from her soon-to-be-running vintage feat: a Unique Thrift Store and two others, a St. Vincent de Paul location and two other unmarked, seemingly abandoned junk/thrift shops, their windows packed tight with children's highchairs, discolored dinette sets, broken bicycles, broken breakfronts, etc. Everywhere Evelyn looked, she saw incredible amounts of used stuff. George could see only junk that wasn't being turned into much needed dollars, but he trusted Evelyn's vision.

What had they gotten themselves into?

Evelyn was now spinning giddily, indulgently vintage shopping seven days a week. Within a month of their acquiring the building, she had her picking routes and routines down to a retro science. Within a year, she had drilled an enormous hole into this resale block, mining thousands of items in every conceivable collecting category. Envision hitting a vintage gusher: clothing, textiles, jewelry, housewares, furniture, collectibles, toys, whatever. Imagine it all bursting up and out from these many nearby locations and landing back to earth within the confines of Evelyn and George's new storefront, A Vintage Thrift.

Those early years passed as quickly as the dollars and credit card purchases from Evelyn's wallet. From one manic decade and, somehow, well into the next— the years were flying away into some lost vortex of time and treasures.

The routine was constant and unchanged: Evelyn went shopping daily, early and with purpose. She would return with shopping bags full of stuff—often not exceptionally old stuff but generally well-cared-for used things—scooping up whatever she considered items of value. *Someone will certainly want this,* she'd tell herself. It rarely mattered what "this" was, as long as she perceived a value no one else could see. Where others saw "one man's junk," Evelyn mined "one woman's junk addiction."

Now this is not to say that Evelyn didn't occasionally find real antiques—she absolutely did, and the bigger pieces were delivered by those willing or otherwise. She often cajoled a seller into providing free delivery or her potential purchase would not be happening; Evelyn strong-armed many a desperate seller into the free schlep. Some of the better finds included: a 1930s Art Moderne bedroom set with an enormous headboard too large to pass through most doorways; a barbershop's backbar; huge architectural elements; giant metal advertising signage from businesses long gone; and massive stained glass windows from churches long abandoned. These were the exceptions, not the daily finds, yet Evelyn was not about to lose any of her treasures, regardless of the efforts needed to rescue them.

On any given day—and there could be dozens over multiple trips—Evelyn returned to her store again and again with full shopping bags, mostly plastic, some garbage size, some paper grocery bags with those thin paper handles that often broke, there being nothing worse than breaking things that were already half-broken.

George did his share of filling up the place, as well, but not like Evelyn. No one was like Evelyn. Bags and ever more bags, at first by the dozens, then hundreds, then thousands, then beyond any conceivable count filled every possible corner. Furniture and larger items, such as sewing machines, beauty-salon chairs, vintage appliances, dental cabinets, and the entire contents of a gynecological clinic would all be buried, covered, and smothered in the daily deluge of Evelyn's shopping bags.

Like any addiction, it had started slowly, the fun of it all blinding one from the danger ahead, the sheer scale of the growing hoard spawning into every available space like an infection in search of a host. Evelyn often referred to it as inventory. Yet, over time, George would find himself deciding: "All this stuff has snuck up our ass!"

***

Decades in the Unmaking
Over the course of its first decade and stumbling well into an overstuffed second, A Vintage Thrift was overstocked, over-schlocked, and never inventoried. Bags might be sorted or repackaged into other bags—drapery, bark

cloth, textiles—and some vintage clothing was rebagged and simply shoved in the attic. But the buying continued, and the endless flow of bags never slowed down for long. A lifetime of shopping gradually filled this giant A-frame from basement to attic and apartments in between with ever more bags.

Evelyn followed the discount routines of her fellow next-door neighbor—Unique Thrift Stores and their color-coded days of extra discounts cum value—which equaled, of course, more bags.

Through it all, George tried to keep the building—and most important, Evelyn—with the funds she needed to shop. But like most of his life, his personal income resulted from less-than-stellar real estate investments and businesses—a car wash in neighborhood where few people owned cars, a hot dog stand in area that had transitioned into being heavily Jewish . . . You get the unprofitable picture.

George, now in both failing health and judgment, juggled multiple mortgages, refinancing what he could, taking on second mortgages, third mortgages, and re-refinancing his refinancing. His liabilities, as well as those of Evelyn's, had become titanic. Their mutual credit card debts alone were over $100,000, all painfully accruing atmospherically high interest.

This, however, was only what George knew. Whatever else Evelyn had purchased by means both possible and impossible, questionable or not: Evelyn was broke, if not broken. And George had helped her do it.

One night in the late 1990s, George passed in his sleep in the back apartment of A Vintage Thrift: Buy and Sell. He was found spread on top of a pile of shopping bags, tightly holding a single plastic handle. Even in his death, it appeared he'd been dreaming of moving those damn bags.

Evelyn soon relocated into a senior facility, which was a bit of a handful for anyone with hands to help her, and she lived for few more years. She started a holiday rummage sale for the "inmates and guests." By the time she passed, her little room had once again filled up with the "valuable" stuff she'd purchased at the nursing home. Some things never change.

To this end, it was all a long and cluttered trip to nowhere. Carrying all those bags and treasures found that had been more displaced than lost. Evelyn's resale dreams had been a burden to them both, carried through the passing years, the doubling of decades, all filled with the "wait and see," the "wait and find."

Find she did. In her time, Evelyn found a million little moments of her treasure hunter's life. Her ecstasy was the find, the collectible climax of a rather thrifted lust, a never-satiated sale of satisfaction.

***

2015: The Bag Man

For those of you wondering what happened to their venture, A Vintage Thrift: Buy and Sell never materialized in the resale/retail world. No items ever priced. No vintage merchandise ever displayed. Perhaps most incredibly, their store door ever opened. Ever. Twenty-plus years in the making, it was all blue balls and boner killers in the end, a sort of resale foreplay never to be finished off.

Like some retro-hoarding house of cards, the collapse came, and the business—if one could ever truly call it a business—was sadly gone.

When I arrive at the old building, I am met by a giant red dumpster parked outside at the curb. Empty. Whew. The store's front door has been crudely pried open, a crowbar lay nearby, and half a dozen young men, many in hazmat suits, lumber in and out faster and faster, like ants at a rotting picnic. Except these ants each hold shovels. Yes, they were all shoveling bags, hundreds of shopping bags.

The dumpster fills slowly with, well, a lot of dirt, actual dirt; it's a weird soil-like mixture of newspaper, scraps of clothing, garbage, feces, many a dead rodent, human hair, and broken everything. But mostly plastic bags, chewed and shredded and many strangely empty.

As if on a bizarre forensic expedition, the clean-out crew begins separating the unrecognizable into the recognizable. An unwieldy floor-to-ceiling hoard features boxes and bundles running up from one side of the room to the other: a seemingly bottomless black hole of trash.

After a few hours, a path is finally dug through the room, zigzagging to the back of the store—the hoard still waist-/waste-high—and the cleanout crew can nearly navigate their steps without fear of falling into an unsorted and potentially dangerous pile of trash. Finally, the room comes into scattered focus, and we can see what is to be tossed or salvaged to recycle or resell. We wade through and step over, into, and atop even more piles of bags, slowly, carefully opening each to reveal those items discovered by Evelyn but never permitted to be rediscovered by anyone else.

After many an exhausting day, most of A Vintage Thrift is finally whittled down to assorted filing cabinets, shelving units, dead wooden radios, rotary telephones, chrome fans, a pair of nightstands, some old tools, a baby doll, and a disturbingly realistic paper-mache clown. Multiple dumpsters haul away the contents of the store and the parallel hoard in the basement. Had the bank not demanded the building be emptied before its demolition, everything would have met the swing of the wrecking ball.

Whereas the store yields little in the way of treasure, the second-floor apartments and attic prove a bit more satisfying. Here, the good stuff turns out to be things not rare or particularly valuable but the contents of a life—two, in fact. Antique furniture from the 1920s, a deco dining table and matching chairs, sconces and fixtures still wired to the ceiling, table and floor lamps, pottery and glass, and a staggering amount of kitchen and housewares: Pyrex bowls, decorative sets of kitschy glassware, and Bakelite serving utensils by the handfuls.

Nearing the end of sorting both apartments, I find a beautiful full-length mink coat, nearly new, which obviously belonged to Evelyn. Laying it gently on top of a small mountain of rescued items, I take a deeper dive into the closet of its origin but find only a few additional pieces: a small travel case, a Marshall Field's hatbox, and a brand-new leather handbag. Yet when I bring the items to my pile of treasures, the mink coat is gone. One of the cleanout crew must have absconded with the coat. Or perhaps Evelyn was having some fun with me from the great resale beyond. No matter, it's gone, and one should never cry over fur that has been flung, especially if it's out a window to a thieving accomplice below.

As if on an anthropological dig, I can't help but notice nearly fifty different phone numbers scrawled across the kitchen wall. Many have been written in different color inks and handwritings; some numbers are carved into the wall itself, perhaps with a knife. Strangely, the old dial wall phone is gone, but that isn't what draws me to this odd clue. Beside the multiple numbers, the letter "F" appears countless times, as if a curious code.

I ask a few of the cleanout crew guys what they know of these urban hieroglyphics. Casually, they relate that after George and Evelyn had lost the building to the bank, it was abandoned yet again, and pimps had moved in and set up a crack house. The phone numbers are the working girls' clients. And only hours earlier, I'd questioned the need for hazmat suits.

Like a rotting time capsule, great will fall to good; good will fall to mediocre; and mediocre will fall to, well, garbage. Time takes its toll on everyone and, in this instance, everything.

My last attack is the attic: the giant A-frame splits the high-ceilinged room into two great sides, where huge black garbage bags are stacked high, parting the hoard like Moses on an off day, dividing the Red "See what a great deal I got today?" A path now separates two enormous, evenly placed black walls of bags.

This may sound peculiar, but in this last claustrophobic room, I am reminded of Andy Warhol and his similarly bizarre purchasing habits. Andy was famous for his shopping excursions through various flea markets in Manhattan or wherever his travels would take him across the globe. After his untimely death, hundreds of his purchases—most still in their original shopping bags—were found throughout the units of Warhol's apartment building. Many had never been opened. Much later, these purchases would be auctioned off to create the Andy Warhol Foundation for the Visual Arts; however, I doubt that had ever been his intent while scouring New York's famous 26th Street Flea Market in Chelsea. There, he scored fantastic art deco items, being especially fond of cigarette cases, Bakelite jewelry, and his iconic cookie jars.

Oh, and he always got a deal. "I don't know," Andy was often heard complaining to the flea market dealer in question. Whatever the asking price, he would lament like some resale parrot: "That seems like a lot of money. Can't you do any better?" And, of course, they did.

In a trashy fashion, was Evelyn really that different from Andy Warhol? They both coveted vintage in a nearly identical manner: shopping seemed to be their "high," while unpacking shopping bags was a disinterested "low." Uncontrollable, obsessive, driven, compulsive, and in their own respective ways, perhaps brilliantly mad.

In the end, it was all about the stuff, until it wasn't. And don't we all carry our respective baggage—both figuratively and literally, plastic, recyclable paper, or otherwise—until it's all too much?

The difference, I would guess, is the scale and final sale of one's remaining mess.

CHAPTER 20

MR. PEANUT, FAMED SPOKESNUT AND HOLLYWOOD LOTHARIO, UNSHELLED AT 104

On January 23, 2020, the legendary Mr. Peanut was killed in an ill-conceived, badly timed marketing ploy by a wayward advertising agency. The death occurred during the filming of an ill-conceived, badly timed Super Bowl ad that has since been viewed six million times, mostly by mistake.

The good news: commercial costar Wesley Snipes was paid handsomely for his part in this debacle. The bad news: the IRS has since confiscated Snipes's earnings for back taxes and lost eyeliner revenue.

Mr. Peanut had a storied but tumultuous career with the Planters organization, his longtime employer and corporate pimp. Initially introduced to the public through quaint print ads and later dancing with his trademarked top hat and cane on television and film, he ascended smoothly to a near iconic status of Americana. Mr. Peanut's peanut buttery goodness was a staple both in the industry and in grocery store aisles, often seen alongside his partner, Jelly; his nemesis, Bread; and his ex-wife, Cold Milk, who he often unaffectionately referred to as "curdled."

But this was only one side of the public peanut: stylish and dapper, an elegant dandy, the life of the party . . . and often, a profiting allergist's dream. In fact, it is said his mere scent singlehandedly financed innumerable 1stDibs purchases, various second homes, and countless third facelifts.

Still, most of the public was unaware of Mr. Peanut's dark backstory, the man inside the shell, the unroasted truth. Shockingly, the private Peanut's tale would prove to be near unspeakable, if not unrepeatable, as the telling of his story often slowed the most gossipy of buttered mouths.

Much like the infamous Joan Crawford/Betty Davis feud, Mr. Peanut had many longstanding disagreements with Monopoly's Rich Uncle Pennybags, mostly because neither could sit—hence their mutual use of a cane, often on each other's backsides. Once considered a peculiar peccadillo, today there are Subreddit groups for this specific interest, and we no longer judge.

Sadly, Mr. Pennybags was unavailable for comment, as he is now part of the former Trump administration, being used as an uncomfortable ottoman in Steve Mnuchin's gold-plated office. Pennybags's upcoming memoir, *Where's My $400 Million, Bitch?*, will be released only in audiobook format, as soon as we can decipher his confused mutterings. Apparently, he holds no monopoly on elocution.

Mr. Peanut had only recently discovered, via a 23andMe test, that his father was the actor Ed Asner (the similarity is eerie), and his mother—in one of her less thoughtful decisions—the actress Betty White. Peanut's conception occurred during a dinner break while filming *The Mary Tyler Moore Show*'s classic "Chuckles Bites the Dust" clown episode. Yes, Asner's irresistible good looks and consoling demeanor turned Betty White's frown upside down. And then he worked on her face.

Mr. Peanut is survived by hundreds of thousands of children and one jar of Skippy Super Chunk that has refused to take a DNA test, even on the Maury Povich show. Dr. Phil offered to conduct the test in the Dr. Phil house, directly beside the Dr. Phil garage, which is next to the Dr. Phil pool cabana, but Skippy Super Chunk would not agree to the complimentary make-over or the eternal youth face mask serum application. Needless to say, Skippy's chunky skin remains not so smooth. His loss.

As a young sprout, Mr. Peanut was alleged to have had affairs with countless starlets, going back to the silent film days . . . mostly because he was a terrible conversationalist. "Look! I have no pants!" was his pickup line of choice at the time and, surprisingly, it usually worked. He had liaisons with such cinematic icons as Mary Pickford, Gloria Swanson, Lillian Gish, and Jadaan, Rudolph Valentino's prized Arabian stallion. (Hey, it was the 1920s!)

Later, Peanut would plant himself within such beauties as Greta Garbo, Lana Turner, Katharine Hepburn, and Roy Rogers's horse, Trigger. (Hey, it was the 1940s!)

During the late sexy 1960s, Mr. Peanut was romancing Jane Fonda, Brigitte Bardot, and Natalie Wood, and he finally settled a long and nasty palipony suit with Mr. Ed. In an odd twist of legal fate, Mr. Peanut was awarded full custody of the actor Alan Young, who would perform as his stunt double in less-than-elegant assignations, such as fluffing the drag hand puppet Madame.

In his later years, Peanut was forced to ride sidesaddle when his quasi-equestrian interests hit the hay. Further humiliation was found when former Mouseketeer and actress Annette Funicello began hawking Skippy Peanut Butter's "nutritional/half the sugar" desirability over Mr. Peanut's former pitch: "Guess what else gets stuck to the roof of your mouth?"

Now, with his personal life in a steep decline, Mr. Peanut began to drink, usually cheap beer at dive bars, often consuming vast amounts of cocktail peanuts. Yes, sadly, shockingly, at the end of his life, he became a drunken, peanut-eating cannibal.

And what of George Washington Carver's remaining three hundred uses for the ever-adaptable peanut? Well, Mr. Peanut was far and away his greatest discovery, unless of course it turns out peanuts can cure cancer. Then, never mind.

Regarding Mr. Peanut's legendary libido, one thing is now disturbingly clear: he was the Orson Welles of his time, plowing pertinent starlet fields both on and off the farm. In an odd twist of Hollywood history, Welles's long-lost cinematic exposé on the life of Mr. Peanut,

Citizen Top Hat & Cane, has never been found . . . even in the well-stocked snack aisle of your local 7-Eleven.

In lieu of flowers, Mr. Peanut's personal assistant, Jam, has requested the public embrace "legume-enlightenment" and refrain from using the politically incorrect phrase "kick in the nuts." Today, we recognize this to be what it truly is, peanut hate speech.

CHAPTER 21

TALES OF THE MONKEY GIRL

And then there was the time I took a one-eyed girl to a 3D movie. This is not a joke—it actually happened. No, I wasn't being an insensitive jerk, not intentionally at least. I just wasn't paying attention to an important detail, namely someone's vision.

In my defense—and on an erotic lark—my friend Jane and I thought it would be an adventure to attend a screening of the film *Eruption* starring the infamous John Holmes of porno fame. The flick was not being shown in some seedy grind house but rather at Chicago's Music Box Theatre, a small but opulent cinema from yesteryear, as part of an art film series.

Not exactly an exhibition for the trench coats of the beholders.

"Just imagine how huge John Holmes will be on the big screen?" I squealed. "His face is tough to look at, but . . ."

"Oh," Jane cooed, "say no more. I am in!"

Snagging our popcorn and diet sodas and settling into the half-filled, soon-to-be obscene theatre, it was hard not to feel just a tad naughty as we awaited the blue opus. Only the night before, the theatre had showcased *Gone with the Wind*, yet here we sat with expectation of something equally blow worthy.

I handed Jane her 3D glasses. She handed me a puzzled look but said nothing. We both donned the plastic goggles in apprehension, and within the very first frames, our troubles rightly began.

Jane elbowed me with a "WTF? It's all blurry!"

"What?" I whispered back as the credits began.

"I can't fuckin' see a fuckin' thing!"

Behind us, someone whispered a rightful *"Shush,"* but our bickering continued.

"What do you mean you can't see? Fix your glasses!"

"I can't see, dipshit. It's 3D!"

"I know it's 3D. It was filmed in 3D."

"But I'm blind in one eye . . ."

"So what?"

"So fucking what? I can't see in 3D, that's what!"

"Oh . . ."

"Yeah, damn straight, oh!"

I immediately felt awful. Honestly, I still do. But in the moment, all I could think to do was to narrate the action on the screen for her as softly as possible. Without detailing the audible screenplay, suffice it to say that my verbal subtitles did not stand up to the limp storyline.

When it came to—how do I phrase this?—the climax of the film, John Holmes shot his trademark "Johnny Wadd" into the audience, or more accurately, seemingly above the heads of the anxiously awaiting spectators. A hundred-plus barely aroused people now screamed in mass-participatory delight, many holding their hands out to block the faux splooge that wasn't actually shooting into the air, hysterically laughing in shocked, if not disgusted, amazement.

Years later, Blue Man Group would make millions with this gimmick, but truth be told, Holmes Sherlocked this trick first.

But poor Jane, elbowing me for the dozenth time, repeatedly yelled: "What? What-the-fuck? What?"

Yes, when it came time for the money shot, Jane was seriously shortchanged.

This true story rather encapsulates what I loved about her: Jane was tough, street-smart, famously foul-mouthed, and truly fearless. A straight single woman, she called the shots not only with the challenges in her life but her men as well. She was woman, hear her roar . . . and often with innumerable f-bombs.

We were friends for decades, but this had not always been the case. Oh, not at all. In the beginning, she was my great nemesis. Seriously. I hated her like I hated few others, and I had my reasons. Here's a bit of the backstory.

When I was in my early twenties and starting my first business, I signed a sizable contract with a firm to handle the word processing needs for a group of independent attorneys. Not going into the boringly litigious details of it all, my contract helped settle some contractual troubles of the landlord. To be blunt, I was fulfilling the obligations of a prior company that had gone belly-up. At the time, it was a big deal for me—some $100,000 of business—and I jumped at the chance.

This is when I first met Jane and our feud began.

What I didn't know was that between the time the first company went out of business and I stepped in with my firm, Jane had taken on much of the work from these same attorneys, my future clients. In effect, the contract I signed was Swiss cheese, full of legal loopholes and not nearly as valuable as I was initially told. Though I had rented office space adjacent to my clients, purchased computers, and hired staff based on this contract, in reality, I was now barely holding Swiss cheese curds, if not turds.

To be fair, I would only later learn that none of it was Jane's fault. She had simply been there first: whip smart, "a paralegal's paralegal," and far more accomplished—dare I say *professional*—than I was at the time. She could type and talk faster than anyone I'd met before or since. Jewish and an ex–New Yorker, she would wisecrack with her disarming rat-a-tat accent of whine and momma roses, dropping Yiddish vernacular like a Borscht Belt comic on a bender. Bring on the hecklers: it was Jane's legal show. She was just that good.

Over the years, Jane worked for many an accomplished, high-powered Chicago attorney and politician, maneuvering her career between the inflated and often sensitive egos of powerful men. She was a tough talker who took no bullshit, especially in the male-dominated area of law and often lawlessness.

When Jane began taking on "my" clients, she was working full-time for Sam, an old-time lawyer who could have represented John Wilkes Booth if he hadn't ruined his acting career with that one bad review at Ford's Theatre. Where Jane was a mile-a-minute personality, Sam lived by the slowly passing hour: thoughtful, considerate, yet always adding to his billables. I would soon discover as much about Sam and Jane as I would about myself.

You see, early on I'd learned that being litigious wasn't a good idea, and I learned it the hard way: yes, from being litigious myself. For starters, one should rarely sue an attorney. It costs them nothing to defend themselves, unlike your soon-to-be legally debt-driven self. Attorneys will pay their ten-dollar court fee to file their defense, yet you'll have an attorney on retainer who's charging you for every lick of a postage stamp.

Still, in my present quagmire, I knew I had no legal recourse. None. I needed a solution, and I needed it fast . . . and it wouldn't be found in the courts.

Of course, I started with Jane and attempted to explain that my contract explicitly stated the attorneys I was to work with: attorneys whose work she was currently doing. It did not go well. While typing in a whirlwind and barely looking in my direction, she smiled coyly and said: "I couldn't give two shits about your contract!"

Okay, not the answer I was expecting. Round one: Jane.

We went back and forth for a few minutes, her fingers rattling off her one-hundred-plus words a minute, while only having two for me, and they weren't "Happy Hanukkah."

The next day, I asked Jane whether I could make an appointment to see her boss, Sam. Smiling once again—oh, that devilishly cute smile, those darn brown eyes—she put me into Sam's appointment calendar. I was certain I could explain the nature of the matter and that we could amicably resolve this situation.

A few days later, I sat across from Sam in his office, an unpretentious and tidy room, notably devoid of clutter, most likely due to Jane's efficiency. I made my case as simply as possible: I signed a contract with building management to provide exclusive legal services to their tenants. The contract explicitly detailed which attorneys I would work with and the hourly rate I would charge. The attorneys didn't care who did their work, as long as it was done accurately and expeditiously. No issues from them.

Sam listened to my plea then explained his side of things, replying: "You'll need take this up with building management. If Jane wants to do their work on the side, that's her prerogative. I certainly have no problem with it. To me, it sounds like the building presented you with something they weren't at liberty to offer."

Hmm. For as much as I disliked his words, Sam had a point. Still, the building management was my landlord, as well, and suing them to fulfill a contract seemed as pointless as suing an attorney. I was screwed.

Sam continued: "I can see you have a problem. Perhaps your contract isn't as profitable as you had hoped? Perhaps there's another way around this? How many attorneys are we talking about here? Forty? Fifty? Jane couldn't possibly make that big a dent in your new business. Besides, you're new here. Always best to try making friends first, enemies later." He shook my hand firmly and directed me back to Jane's desk.

For the first time, Jane stopped typing. She was waiting for the word, perhaps a war, or possibly a resolution.

"I have an idea," said Sam, sitting on the corner of Jane's desk. "You need to work this out together. I can arbitrate a framework, but you guys have to flesh out a business truce and move forward. Why don't the two of you go out for a drink tonight? Talk about the matter. Get to know one another. I don't think it's really a problem unless you both decide to make it one."

Jane perked up. She looked over the top of her computer's monitor and, without missing a beat, said, "We good?" I nodded. "Great!" She rebounded with, "There's a mediocre bar in the basement of the building. Have you been?"

"Well, I'm not much of a drinker, but . . ."

"Great!" she finished, ignoring my response. "See you at five thirty. Oh, and I like Black Russians, the cocktail, not the ethnicity."

Boom. Round two: Jane.

Sam stood up, clearly uncomfortable with the joke, then offered: "I think you two will be just fine together."

His comment would prove to be profitably prophetic. In so many ways, that evening at the bar was a turning point. As for splitting up the word processing work, by the second round of cocktails—Jane with Black Russians, me with White—the pieces of our problematic legal puzzle fell into perfect place.

Jane had her favorite attorneys, and she wouldn't budge with those clients, at least for now. But as for the troublemakers, the late payers, and especially the skirt chasers—of which there were many—they were all mine. In fact, by cocktails/round three and beyond, I learned more than any business plan or contract could ever have detailed.

Over the following year, not only would Jane give me her overflow work, I gave her mine. And we worked together on a myriad of projects; there were always last-minute changes of wills to be made, signature pages updated, witnessing to be done, and real estate closings to be processed. Together we profited, not only financially but personally. As the years progressed, we laughed at how some dumb and distant dispute could birth such an unlikely friendship.

When I turned thirty, I decided to walk away from the legal word processing biz; I was sick of screaming lawyers and glaring computer screens—and proofing the shoddy work of the countless college kids I'd hired from a nearby business school. My favorite Latin mistranslation typo: *"duces tecum"* became "douche with a teacup." Now *that* would be some subpoena.

In the end, I was simply sick of myself. Though I was juggling multiple businesses at the time, I was done with this one. But I was never done with Jane nor she with me.

A two-time breast cancer survivor, Jane solicited me annually in support of the Susan G. Komen cancer walk. It was another way in which we had kept in touch over some thirty years of friendship. She'd email me a terse, "Hey, send me money, asshole," and I would. A dinner date would inevitably be set in the weeks that followed, and we'd catch up on the year's events. She called it her "cancer calendar," and it kept us connected over many bumpy decades.

I recall the first time I visited Jane's apartment in the mid 1980s: at the time, she lived close by, and I immediately knew we'd be visiting each other often. However, at that initial visit, I did not expect the monkeys, a great and grand plurality of hundreds—and I do mean hundreds—of monkeys. Monkey art, monkey posters, monkey rugs, monkey furniture (yes, it's a thing), but mostly monkey ceramics: cookie jars, mugs, uncountable figurines, ditto for salt and pepper shakers, not to mention monkey metalware, books, bookends, kitchen utensils, desk accessories, and, of course, clothing. I'm sure I'm forgetting to mention some monkey category because, well, it was all too much!

Jane, pouring 2-percent milk (always on hand just for me) into a glass of Kahlúa and easy on the vodka, would say: "All of my monkeys have to have tails. I mean, monkeys have tails—why they make monkeys without tails is just frickin' ridiculous. I never buy those tailless aberrations, and I hope no one ever does. It's asinine!"

Jane was most serious in this collecting requirement. Every monkey in her collection had a tail. If someone gave her a monkey without a tail, God help their featureless backsides. Into the donate bag it would go.

Now, as luck and monkey fate would have it, around this time I was venturing into the antiques business and finding monkeys hand over, well, tail. I attempted to make mental notes about what monkeys Jane had in her collection—no small feat, given its voluminous size—and she certainly didn't need duplicates in this private zoo. For the most part, I succeeded at surprising her with new additions to her collection for birthdays, holidays, or no reason at all. And when I opened my first antiques store, she was quick to snatch up any random monkey she didn't already own from my dealer-tenants. A win-win.

Over time, both of us bought our respective condominiums, and Jane moved downtown into a large two-bedroom corner unit, taking her menagerie with her. I remained in Chicago's Lakeview neighborhood in a classic MCM high-rise. We frequently dined together, often chatting about her work, my work, life, the men in our lives, the life in our men, etc. And, of course, monkeys.

Jane was the consummate collector, and though I knew countless other collectors who could drone on for hours about their vinyl LPs, railroad lanterns, lady head vases, paperweights, advertising rulers, hatpins, cocktail shakers, military memorabilia—all obsessions lost in the obscurity of time and, occasionally, my lessening interest—Jane and her monkeys never bored me. Perhaps it was because I loved her; perhaps it was because she so genuinely loved me back.

On one disturbing Friday afternoon, Jane told a coworker she wasn't feeling well; she was never one to complain, so her comment was more than worrisome. The coworker encouraged her to leave work early and stop at the nearby immediate care facility on her way home as a precaution. Apparently, she did not. Jane was as stubborn in life as she was loyal to her work ethic; her life had always been lived on her terms, and so it would be.

The following Monday, she didn't come into the office—totally unlike her—and the same coworker called her sister. Jane's condominium staff did a wellness check and discovered, sadly, shockingly, that she had passed over the weekend.

I recall receiving the news in a rather obligatory "Where-when-why-what-the-fuck?" fashion. The details really didn't matter. My friend, my one-time nemesis, was dead. Whatever the answers that might later come now seemed unimportant, and whatever could be explained away, or better still, simply denied, remained moot.

Still, an answer would be revealed: a few days after Jane's passing, her family was informed about a serious local flu that had been making the rounds in Chicago, and this, tragically, was what had happened. The illness came on fast and fatally; Jane became an early victim to this mini epidemic. She was too young, and her death came as a shock to us all.

A few weeks later, Jane's sister called and asked me to help process her estate. This was extremely difficult, given our decades-long friendship, but I did as I was asked. I must confess that selling the objects of a stranger's estate is, for the most part, easy. One has zero connection or emotions to the items to be processed. But for a friend, especially a close friend, it's a painfully difficult experience. I could empathize with Jane's sister and her family members because I, too, felt I was part of her extended family. Every item's destiny was now a decision to be made—big, small, and every tailed object in between—by me.

Thankfully, Jane's sister and her partner took care of many issues. I brought in a friend to sell the apartment—which was truly spectacular—but over the passing of many months, the unit could not find a buyer. Other units in the building with the same layout, same tier, lower floors, and for more money, had all sold. Something just wasn't right in this zoo.

One night over dinner, my realtor/friend explained the problem: the unit had now sat unsold for far too long, not a single offer, even after a price drop. And as we all know, it's hard to turn around a stale property.

I thought about this for some time, finally deciding on an odd solution to this problem. "Jane knows who's going to get this apartment—or maybe, who *isn't*," I offered. "Stubborn in life, I'd guess even more stubborn on the other side, but she still knows what she wants. Now, this may sound strange, but after the next open house, after everyone has left, you need to talk to her. Tell her that her sister can't keep paying the monthly assessments, and a new, higher property tax bill is on its way; she'll understand that. Talk to her as if she's there, because she is. She needs to let the apartment go—her home was her everything."

And finally, as if in a delineated revelation, I said, "It's her house of monkeys. They all need to go on to future homes, to be found and adopted once again."

I still shudder just a tad whenever I relate this story. The following week, the realtor went back to the unit for yet another open house, easily his tenth attempt. But now, regardless of how hard he tried, he could not open the front door; the lock tumblers turned, but the keys would not open the door. He tried for over twenty minutes, angry with himself and this strange situation. Frustrated, the realtor headed to the elevator: people were waiting downstairs, and he'd have to cancel the open house. But just as the elevator got to the floor, my friend thought: *I've got to try this locked door one more time.* So he asked Jane to give him a break—his very words—and, just like that, effortlessly, the door opened.

The realtor hosted this open house, but no immediate offers were forthcoming. Once again, he spoke to Jane within the confines of the apartment. He even had his partner—a lovely but rather reluctant Greek—talk to her as well. They paraphrased what I told them to say. Knowing them, they were probably kinder than I would have been given the desperate circumstances. Still, whatever they said seemed to invoke a powerful response from Jane herself.

At this last showing, one realtor had come without her client, which in itself was rather odd. She took a few photos and shot a quick video. That night, she sent the images off to her client and—sight unseen—her client offered the exact sales price Jane's sister had agreed to sell it for. No negotiations. Done.

I don't know who purchased the unit, and I don't need to know. However, I am most certain Jane knows because Jane decided. She was still calling the shots, Kahlúa be damned.

While trying to find a buyer for Jane's apartment, I took on the task of processing the hundreds of items that comprised her estate. The newer monkey items were donated to various charity thrifts, while the vintage monkeys were sold at my shop, many of which had originated there via Jane's many purchases.

Over time, my staff and I realized that if we talked about Jane—and it had to be in an almost accidentally casual, nondeliberate way, such as remembering her favorite restaurant or band or making a joke about vodka—we would sell a monkey.

Now, we couldn't actively make it happen; it had to be by chance. And per her sister's request, Jane's monkeys—nearly each and every tail—found their homes, one by one. I only wished that Jane's family could have seen how happy those monkey collectors became when they adopted one of Jane's most precious monkeys—the joy in their eyes, in Jane's eyes.

My last duty for the estate should have been the easiest, but it certainly was not. I told her sister of a most worthy cause that could handle the enormous amount of Jane's clothing that needed to be donated. Sarah's Circle is a venerable Chicago charity that provides professional clothing to homeless and abused shelter women so they can seek employment.

Years earlier, I had donated my late Aunt Bernice's clothes, and I knew the facility would give each woman a dress, coat, shoes, and perhaps a handbag. My aunt had been quite the fashion plate, so I imagined many a fantastic makeover leaving the Sarah's Circle Uptown facility: women who moved into their new lives empowered by the fine threads of my late relative's exceptional style.

Today, however, would be markedly different, if not much more difficult. Times had changed. Though I had an appointment to donate, I was met at the door by a security guard who was very clear about their No Men Allowed policy. Apparently, husbands and boyfriends would occasionally show up to cause trouble, hence the guard. And even though I had donations to make—and clothing exactingly suitable for those in need—they would not accept the dozen-plus heavy bags of business clothing I had lugged from my car to the vestibule.

I chatted with the guard for some time and asked to speak to someone/anyone connected with the organization. After considerable schmoozing, the guard told me to wait. Within the hour, he returned with a young woman who was most pleasant but still adamant about not accepting donations that day; they were short-staffed, very busy, no time to sort these things, no one to move bags, etc.

Finally, after relating an abbreviated version of the above story, the young woman relented. With the guard still at my side, I dragged the many bags of Jane's beautiful business clothing that represented a lifetime of professional attire through the large metal doorway and onto a high concrete landing.

In a distant room below, I saw a long line of women waiting to be given their new/donated clothing. I watched as the women were taken one by one into a small cage-like clothing store set up at the back of the shelter. Here, each was given her choice of new-for-them, appropriate office attire. I noted bins parallel to the gated door entrance: for nylons, undergarments, and lastly, should the woman so desire, a handbag of her choosing.

At the very front of the line, I spotted the profile of a woman who looked familiar. She stood stooped, looking tired and pale, and patiently waited. Her clothes were simple, sad thrift store finds. Then, as if on cue, she suddenly turned and looked squarely up at me, her lips curving and half smiling. Our eyes met, and I did a cinematic double take. I blinked, and my mouth went instantly dry. I stared, feeling my eyes bulge out in that fashion that only disbelief implores.

Here was Jane's doppelganger. Thinner, clearly besieged by life and her current situation, but the color and cut of hair, her face, the coy smile. It wasn't Jane, of course, but her unmistakable twin in another lifetime, in another circumstance and here for another chance to take and turn around her life.

I could only pray: *Another monkey girl.*

CHAPTER 22

A JOYLESS SPARK

Presently, this is a work of fiction. Only the translations have been changed to protect the recyclables.

Donald Trump, Marie Kondo, and her interpreter walk into a bar . . . Okay, to be fair, Marie does not simply *walk into a bar*, she actually leaps through the bar's doorway while releasing a small squeal of animated delight. Her female interpreter follows glumly behind, a loyal union of one.

But Donald Trump walks into the bar as if conquering the 21 Club at happy hour. He crosses the room with grand aplomb, his Trump Signature Collection tie dragging across the lackluster floorboards, immediately recognizing the shabbiness of the establishment.

"Maria Tidy?" Trump misnames the cult cleaning author and personality. "So this is where you wanted to meet?" He waves his arms about in distress. "This place feels like Studio 53½ before the hookers arrive!"

"Hai—koko nara umaku ikudeshou," Marie replies with a sly smile.

The interpreter turns to Trump: "Yes, this will do nicely."

Trump glances about the bar's interior with a face of distaste . . . or perhaps it was just McGas. "This dump looks like the Hillary Clinton pizza joint Sean Hannity warned me about in my nightly lullaby. But if this is what you want, I'll get us the very best table—the finest—something made of wood or at least near the window. The feds are always watching, ya know."

"Totemo yoidesu."

"You two are very cute too!" Trump drools as he plops his sizable self onto a small bistro chair.

Marie and the interpreter stand momentarily, half expecting their chairs to be gentlemanly pulled out for them, but soon realize their social miscalculation.

"Reigi ga arimasen ne," the interpreter whispers to Marie as they settle in. Marie sparks a small giggle.

Trump is oblivious, his eyes wandering about his surroundings in a panicked search for a camera, any camera. Or paraphrasing Madonna: "Why would you say something if it's off camera?"

"So, Maria," Trump reluctantly begins without the benefit of media. "I'm told you're a best-selling author and television star. That's really great. Not as great as me, myself, and I-can't-believe-I'm-in-this-dive, but then whoever will be again, right?"

"Anata ni aete koei, todemo itte okimashouka," Marie snarks with a smile.

"It's an honor to meet you." The interpreter half laughs, leaving the word "almost" out of Marie's greeting.

Growing bored, Trump attempts to sit back in his chair, but it creaks like the falling of a wooden Floridian rollercoaster. "You know," he boasts, "I wrote the best best-selling book in history, *The Art of the Deal.*" He snorts an energizing sniff. "You know my book outsold the Bible—and even in heathen countries like Chy-na. No offense to such an unfortunately flat-chested woman such as yourself, of course."

"Watashitachi wa nihonjin desu!" Marie corrects, her interpreter simultaneously echoing: "We are Japanese!"

"Really? You sure? What the shit?" Trump scoffs. "You know, I never, ever use foul language. I'm probably the least foulmouthed person you'll ever meet. Now, when I say 'foul,' I mean 'fowl.' Many people tell me this. In fact, Frank Purdue sat on my cabinet but mostly because we ran out of chairs."

Marie and her interpreter trade befuddling glances, but Trump continues: "I know all the best words, words that know each other, or at least heard of themselves in a passing sentence. And speaking of a passing sentence: Did you know I'm the only person I know who hasn't been convicted of a crime?"

As the interpreter attempts to convey Trump's incoherence, Marie's happy demeanor slowly fades from her typically cheery face into a deep dourness.

Trump flags down a less-than-willing waiter. "Let me get you ladies a drink or two; you both look thirsty—and hot."

The interpreter jumps in: "Tea with lemon, please. Anything other than Lipton, if possible."

"So you don't like our American tea?" Trump quizzes. "When you're in America, you should be drinking American tea."

Marie rolls her eyes as if she's lost a contact lens.

"Baka!" The interpreter gasps. "Mister former-still-ex-defeated-president Trump, Lipton is a *British* tea, a fine tea, but not one to our tastes."

Trump sighs. "I don't think any of that is true, but . . . whatever. It's your fake tea bagging."

"Katazuke wo shitainodesuka?" Marie inquires.

"There she goes with the dirty language again!" Trump wheezes dramatically. "Incredible! Your TV show must be on MSNBC after Rachel Mad at Me. There's no swearing on Fox, you know; it's usually just Steve Doocy having an alphabetic Soviet seizure; that man sure loves his vowels."

The interpreter interjects: "No. Marie said 'I understand you wish to do some tidying up.' You've a big mess, yes?"

"It's the Jewish-hating Democrats!" blurts Trump, frightening the bubble gum remnants from the bottom of their pub table. "They're the mess! Biden's a mess. Nancy Pelosi's a mess. Chuck Schumer's a mess. And that Alexis Occasion-Cortez, well, she's a hot mess. Very hot but still a mess. And as for me: I'm just *great*. No collusion. No insurrection. I beat COVID with a quick helicopter ride from a mental hospital. In fact, many people say I'm the greatest living president still living. I'm also told I'm taller and thinner than I am in person. And vice versa. No Kremlin kidding."

The interpreter attempts to repeat Trump's bloviated rant without losing consciousness.

Marie tries to listen intently but then simply shakes her head in frustration at Trump's unwoven fabrications and other polyblend problems.

"Marie has seen this before." Her aide exhales. "Nixon, Clinton, Ethel and Julius Rosenberg. You *really* need some supersized tidying up."

"Nixon was a hero!" Trump shouts into the muddled conversation. "Putin told me this most strongly while I was serving him breakfast in Belgrade . . . and I believe him. In fact, I've seen Nixon's face on the backside of Roger Stone. It's not just a tattoo; it's very lifelike. In fact, I once saw the lips move. Just don't ask me what I was doing at the time, but let me tell you . . . that's one honest face."

Marie nods in weary acknowledgement at Trump's words. She turns to her interpreter and begins a long, masterful, highly detailed solution to the ex-president's many troubles.

Trump frowns stoically, like a milk of magnesia Mussolini, then waves for the waiter in an attempt to order a Big Mac and Diet Coke. He and the waiter bicker back and forth—the bar can provide the former philanderer-in-chief with a beverage but no burger— and Trump grows increasingly unhinged.

"Let me be clear," he begins. "Trump Tower Moscow would have been the largest Mickey D's in the world. My Moscow Hamburglar would've been *so* powerful he wouldn't have needed to wear a mask while spreading COVID-19 at a Leningrad Trump rally."

Marie suddenly starts blessing every corner of the room, everywhere except where she now finds herself trapped.

Trump continues: "And then I'd build a huge, impenetrable wall around the deep fryer—no brown splatter whatsoever. I'd bring back Freedom Fries without any of that artery-clogging socialism. And ketchup would remain a vegetable, just as it says somewhere in that Bible I held upside down. Oh, by the wayside, I'm selling Trump-autographed copies of that exact Bible on my website: $6.66 plus $25 shipping/handling. Ivanka and Jared handle all of this when they're not saving the world from the impending Biden-induced zombie apocalypse."

Now the Trumpster fire is on a roll—a Kaiser to be exact, stale and seedless—but the words still stick in his teeth. "So, Ms. Condo or Ms. Co-op or Ms. Rent Control or whatever real estate business you think you're in, I've had my name removed from more buildings than King Tut's first husband."

Marie attempts to refocus The Donald's attentions. *"Tabun anata wa watashitachi ga hajimeru mae ni nomimono wo chumon surubekidesu!"*

The interpreter: "Maybe you should order a drink before we begin." Then to herself: *Cuz you'll need it.*

Ignoring her comment, Trump's tummy rumbles a sound so loudly that it abruptly sets off his unsecured cell phone. Hackers in Malaysia immediately toss off their headphones in pain as the gurgling drones out Trump's usual stereophonic screed of blaming others. His final stomach grumble is so loud it unzips his fly.

And the demands to the waiter just wither on: "I want a Big Mac—or a bucket from the Colonel or Matt Gaetz's underage girlfriend, COVID-17. Oh, and a Diet Coke. Now!"

Turning to the Zen-sorter: "Now, Maria, why the heck did you invite me here today? You think you can fix what isn't broken? Everything is fantastic! I'm fantastic! But okay. If you're so colluded, give it a shot. Ten bucks says Rudy Giuliani screws up whatever you suggest by three o'clock next Thursday!"

Marie looks to her interpreter, who waves Trump off with an SNL-induced Emily Litella "Never mind" and continues: *"Dewa kou shimashou."*

"Here is what you do," Marie exhales via the translator. "First, take all of your problems and make a huge pile on your bed. Perhaps use the master suite at Mar-a-Lago. All of your troubles on the bed . . .

1. the Mueller probe,

2. the Trump International Hotel in DC debacle,

3. the January 6 insurrection,

4. your taxing insurance problems in the Southern District of New York,

5. Michael Cohen's spot-on channeling of John Dean,

6. Mary Trump's book deal, pending film option, and lawsuit,

7. perhaps Don Jr. and Eric because, you know, they're horrible,

8. the entirety of the Republican Party, except Liz Cheney and Adam Kinzinger, because, you know, they're honest,

9. and yes, all of the girlfriends and porn stars you may have lying around as well—you put all on the bed."

"I like the 'chicks in my bed' part," Trump chuckles. "Okay, I'm kinda listening . . . and let's add 'Melania when she wants something.'"

The waiter arrives with tea for the women and a Diet Coke for the ex-president-who-fleeced.

Trump leans toward the waiter and whispers, "The ladies will be picking up the tab . . ."

Marie begins to wave her arms about as if sorting invisible possessions, her gestures moving in arcs from side to side; the interpreter follows her movements Marcel Marceau–like. "Pick up each trouble in your life," Marie politely advises. "Pick up each obstacle and ask yourself if it brings you joy . . . or sadness, water or sky, Dolce or Gabbana . . ."

In mid-sip of his soda, Trump starts to choke. Two Secret Service agents run to the former president's very, very broad side. "I'm fine," he coughs, regaining his "composure."

One agent turns to the other and says, "Stand down! Thank God or the ghost of Rush Limbaugh. I thought we had another gagging George W. Bush salty pretzel incident on our hands."

Marie and her interpreter drink their tea, sullenly assessing the potential subpoena-inducing situation.

Marie speaks, and the interpreter continues: "You must take each issue in your hand and ask if it truly sparks joy in your life. If not, you must dispose of it. But first, thank it for being in your life. Thank each trouble as you would thank your socks."

"Thank my *socks*!" Trump barks, Lassie-like. "Are you nuts? I have people for that. Heck, I think Lindsey Graham has a degree in socks thanking. Or at least ladies' hosiery!" Trump snaps his finger at the waiter. "Hey, how 'bout you freshen up my Diet Coke? This soda fizzled out faster than the Carter administration."

Marie stays the course. "Say, 'Thank you, AOC,' and then put her in a plastic bag for recycling."

Trump suddenly perks up. "Oh my gosh! Tucker Carlson told me the same thing while I watched him resuscitate Rupert Murdoch's corpse on Jeffrey Epstein's jet!"

Marie makes a little bow. "And Michael Cohen. And Rudy Giuliani."

"Who?" Trump asks. "Never heard of them." He pauses, catching sight of his reflection in a nearby mirror, and finds himself getting slightly aroused. "Hey, Maria," he says, adjusting his crotch. "You're all right, a real straight shooter. You know, I've been looking for a new Roy Cohn—but with better legs—and I think you could be it. How do you feel about working at the new-and-improved whiter White House in 2024?"

The interpreter extends the offer to Marie, who softly giggles then wiggles her fingers in the air to snag the waiter's attention. Pointing to her tea, she politely begs: *"Motto ramu."*

Trump leans over, a leering twinkle in his eyes, and asks, "Can I take that as a yes?"

"More rum," pleads the interpreter. The waiter returns and pours the smooth liquid into their steaming cups of tea. "Yes, Marie will require much, much more rum . . ."

"*Excuse* me?" says Trump.

Marie takes a solid swig of her newly improved tea and then spits out in perfect English: "Thank you, no. That won't be necessary. Please save it for—How do you say? Yourself!"

Trump adjusts his thumb-sized junk behind his ridiculously long, overcompensating tie and muddles into his final fascistic pronouncement: "You know, Maria, you're no Bartiromo, and I'm gonna tell you something. At the end of every day—you know it and I know it—everyone is a loser. Every. One. All the women who accused me of the rapes I committed. Losers. The thousands of companies that have sued me for the money I owe them. Losers. The thousands of January 6 protesters who thought I'd be walking over to the Capitol with them. Losers. The hundreds of thousands of people who died of COVID because I told them it was fake news.

Losers. The millions of Republican voters who believed I wouldn't screw them. Losers. All losers, Maria. And you're a loser too. Big time!"

Ms. Kondo stands up from the table, her interpreter rising in unison, and both turn to leave the restaurant. Then, on second thought, she smiles demurely and exhales in perfect English: "Oh yes. Now I understand. Supposedly, you're the savior, but in fact, you're just 'Individual Number One.' Big mess. Two little hands. Three thumbs . . . down."

CHAPTER 23

CZECHS BURIED, NOT BOUNCED

Before my father was drafted into WWII, he snagged an apprenticeship position at his cousin's rather successful printing company. After the war, he was allowed to return and complete this apprenticeship to become a photo engraver. This was some fifty years before computers put a generation or two out of work with specialized software, eventually making my father's profession virtually obsolete. In fact, a quick Google search of his profession now predicts there's a 98 percent chance that robots will replace all photo engravers. I believe if my father were alive today, he'd respond to this claim with one of his own: "Kiss my ass!" Obsolescence may be inevitable for most of us, but it won't be the last foul-mouthed directive from an old Czech.

Though my father was second generation Czechoslovakian, there was an Italian side to the family who were very—how do I say this?—entrepreneurial. My grandfather had been a tailor, worked for Hart Schaffner Marx all his life, and instilled in my father the notion that one should always work for someone else. "Let someone else take the risk," was my family's mantra. Work your hours. Earn a pension. Go the racetrack once a month and the bank once a week. In between, eat as much pork, sauerkraut, and kolackies as ethnically possible.

In the nearby town of Berwyn, Illinois, there was a bank, a restaurant, a bakery, or a funeral home on every downtown corner. Seriously. That was pretty much the resulting architecture and lifestyle of being Czech: Earn. Eat. Save. Die.

The printing company, simply called Superior Graphics, grew and prospered into quite the business, eventually being the production end of Hefner's infamous *Playboy* magazine. The owners, my father's cousin and his wife, quickly became the "wealthy relatives" and soon moved into the ninety-fourth floor of the famous Hancock Building in downtown Chicago. At the time, the Hancock was the tallest residential building in the world. What did this mean?

Even as a child, I was a mere six degrees from bacon's moneyed bacon.

One would think the high-rise view, not to mention the lifestyle, would be unparalleled. Not quite. You see, just one floor above this palatial ninety-fourth-floor slice of homebound heaven was the Signature Room restaurant, then referred to as "the 95th." Sometimes even "The Top of the Cock." Hancock, that is. At such height, dizzy diners could partake in a 360-degree skyscraper view of the dazzling Chicago skyline, Lake Michigan, and beyond. It was said that on a clear day, you could see Milwaukee, Wisconsin, and if that weren't exciting enough, at night you could watch the airplanes land at O'Hare Airport some fifteen miles away. For Chicago, that was some heady entertainment that didn't involve gunfire.

Being the youngest cousin in a family of "alter cockers"—hey, I was the most Jewish Catholic boy that anyone could tolerate—I was always being dragged to the funeral wake of great-aunt fill-in-the-blank. What made any particular aunt "great," I never found out, but the corpses invariably barely fit in any given coffin. For some reason, the Italian side of the family seemed to have more dead relatives than space available in their enormous plot at Bohemian National Cemetery on the north side of Chicago. But, as the horror story often echoes, there was always room for one more.

Like broken clockwork, out from the mothballs would come my routinely recycled black Walt Disney funeral suit, replete with vest, tie, and ever-so-shiny but uncomfortable black shoes. I was never permitted to wear Walt's black hat or my beloved plastic icicles, my mother often making snide Sonja Henie/Peggy Fleming remarks. Ms. Henie, I was told, was Liberace's fiancée, but I'm unsure if such information was an encouragement or a warning. Either way, that path looked icy to me.

Now, it was at one of these all-too-frequent funerals, at which my father's wealthy employer/cousin was always in attendance, that this story happened; the sound of his wife's shrill voice and her duplicitous stories have stayed with me to this day. "It's those damn restaurant bus carts," she'd wail across the organ-humming dirge of the funeral home Muzak. "You can't *believe* the sound those carts make. It's a constant ungodly racket."

Mourners would look up from the recently deceased before breaking into their stereophonic "But-they-did-such-a-nice-job-with-her . . . considering," only to hear her repetitious tirade: "You'd think we'd have it easy, given all the money we pay!" She'd sigh and continue, "But it's 24-7. I've even offered to pay for new wheels for the bus carts or at least grease the old wheels. *Anything.* But those bus boys—the Mexicans—they don't care."

An old woman dropped a used tissue, but her muffled cries barely broke the complaining. The *lamentarsi* continued: "You don't know what real suffering is until you haven't slept for a month. It's killing me, I tell you!"

Even as a child, I half expected the deceased to sit upright in her coffin with a stiff "Seriously, bitch?" By the third wake—Aunty Bellum or some such moniker—my poor rich relative's anguish started to take on the elements of a Mike Nichols/Elaine May skit gone six feet south. "I won't eat there. I just can't!" she informed a row of confused mourners. "Now they refer to me as 'that woman'—can you believe it?—the one who 'hears' the bus carts. Like I'm making it all up!"

Her husband would touch her hand with a knowing numb nudge but say nothing. Now and again, he occasionally rose from his seat to comfort a random mourner, perhaps Uncle Buster's niece from Cicero, the one with a lazy eye. Or the bachelor neighbor Slav who "is probably an 'old mo,'" or so it was rumored in the funeral home's cigarette-clouded lounge.

Typically, I'd remain within distant earshot of my relative's high-anxiety whining, but at the funeral of a suspiciously unnamed spinster relation whose fondness for dumplings was apparently her marital undoing, I had the good misfortune of sitting directly beside the sky-challenged millionaire. What luck for us both. Cue the eye roll. Without prompting, my high-living cousin suddenly confides to me: "Can you believe they had the audacity to tell me to turn up my radio to drown out the sound? Let me tell you, kiddo. That doesn't work; I've tried everything."

Hah! She called me "kiddo" because she didn't even know my name. *This is perfect!*

I muster up my best sad-sack, little-kid whine. "Can you see birds from your windows?" I ask in faux innocence.

"What are you talking about?" she questions, clearly annoyed by my lack of sympathy.

"You live in the clouds," I say. "I bet you can see all kinds of birds."

"They fly right into the windows!" she cries. "They make a terrible screaming sound when they hit the glass and then fall away. All ninety-four floors."

My little face reflects the horror of her statement. "Oh, how awful!" I choke out with a Tony Award–winning whimper.

"But not as awful as those goddamn bus carts! The squeaky-squeaky-squeaks as they roll above my head day and night. I can almost see them move across my ceiling. The crystal drops on my dining room chandelier actually sway when they pass over it. And sometimes the bus carts collide. I hear dishes fall, people cursing, laughing. It's a madhouse, I tell you, a *madhouse!*"

I grab my elderly cousin's hand in a mock concern that only a twelve-year-old can muster. "Why don't you ask your husband if you can move? Like to a lower floor? Or a house where the birds don't die in your windows?"

My mother unexpectedly returns from the closing of the latest coffin lid, sniffling back a tear to an aunt she probably doesn't recall. "Oh, I hope my Duane hasn't said anything . . . well, anything, really."

"Oh, no!" my cousin whimpers back. "He was just suggesting that we should move out of the Hancock Building."

"Children!" says my mother, pulling my hand away from my cousin's like I've just stolen a ring off a corpse . . . again. "He knows *nothing* about real estate! Why, we barely own our own home."

"So is yours a rental unit or a condominium?" I spit out as my mother abruptly pulls me from my seat. "Because if it's a condo, that'll be a tough resale . . ."

I never discovered whether my wealthy cousin moved from the Hancock Building and far from the sound of the bus carts that so distressed her. After what would later be referred to as "the bird-killing incident," I was never again taken to any of the better funerals or funeral luncheons. My pork loin still weeps.

If you think about it, at the time of this tale, my relatives lived higher in the sky than almost any other humans on the planet. Not movie or rock stars or million-aire inventors but a couple who produced magazines chock-full of naked women with platter-sized breasts, coaster-sized nipples, and unwieldy gardens of pubic hair. Still, in the end, my relatives were undone by the rolling carts of busboys who most likely had those same magazines stashed in their work lockers. Today, we also know that somewhere on the 95th menu reads the sweet-est of words: "Just Desserts."

CHAPTER 24

THE GREATEST GENDER-BENDING STAR OF ALL

Here's a fun party game: guess six Broadway theatres named after celebrated Broadway luminaries. Ready?

1. the Gershwin, of George and Ira fame
2. the Helen Hayes, first lady of American theatre
3. the August Wilson

253

4. the Neil Simon

5. the Stephen Sondheim

But who's the sixth? How about Julian Eltinge?
"Who?" you may ask.

Probably the most famous unknown actor who ever died as a famous actress . . . and vice versa.

Let's start with this riveting fact: Dorothy Parker invented the word "ambisexual" to describe Julian Eltinge. Exactly how famous must you be for Dorothy Parker to create a word just for you?

Born in 1881, by the age of ten, Julian Eltinge was appearing onstage in feminine attire and wowing audiences not only with his coquettishly brilliant acting skills but his accomplished vocal abilities. He first appeared on Broadway in 1904 and though hardly an overnight success, his guise as a convincing actress soon began setting box office records on the Vaudeville circuit with his one man/woman parody of the "Gibson Girl" called the "Simpson Girl." European tours brought him international stardom, followed by a fawning Hollywood.

So illuminating a star was Eltinge that legendary theatre architect Thomas W. Lamb designed what he'd hoped would be a lasting edifice to the most famous female impersonator on the planet: the Eltinge. Built in 1912, the beaux arts theatre is still on 42nd Street—well, sort of. The structure was moved some two hundred feet from its original location, where it now serves as the facade and lobby of the AMC multiplex. The lobby remains somewhat intact, with a ceiling fresco detailing the three muses, all Eltinge in elegant lady's attire. Sadly, the artist himself never played at this theatre, but that's only another strange twist in the life and cross-dressing times of Julian Eltinge.

In 1920, Eltinge appeared as a woman (of course) opposite Rudolph Valentino in the silent film *The Isle of Love*, just one of some dozen films in which he would star. Rumors of a bicoastal affair bounced about, although in what gender variance or role reversal of sex/romance no one said, least of all Valentino or Eltinge. Sometimes love is blind, especially when you have a giant bonnet pulled over your wig while singing a tune about virginal splendor.

But who was Julian Eltinge? Though now mostly forgotten, in his time he was one of the most original creations the entertainment world had ever seen: the iconic, one-named wonder: Eltinge! He successfully branded himself with not only a namesake theatre but also a magazine: *The Julian Eltinge Magazine of Beauty Hints*, in which he offered makeup and lifestyle suggestions to his adoring fans of both sexes and sold his own brand of beauty products.

At the height of his fame, Eltinge was one of the highest-paid actors in both film and on the Broadway stage. He parlayed his self-styled musical comedy *The Fascinating Widow* into a financial empire, playing both the smooth-talking college boy and the virtuous virgin—to this day, an acting stretch by anyone's imagination. Consider that some seventy years before the film *Tootsie* would appear as legitimate cross-dressing entertainment fashion, Eltinge had virtually invented the genre.

He somehow seduced both himself and a national audience with an inexplicable yet convincing magic trick of sliding sexuality. Even though the early twentieth century was a more innocent time, people were certainly no more accepting of an LGBTQ pioneer like Eltinge. His perpetually closed closet door did much to shield the public from his private life; however, his overtly feminine, over-the-top public persona was very much the lady fair. Perhaps that same closet door, so filled with gorgeous gowns and fabulous frocks, could never be fully opened against the floodgates of his fashions. In effect, Eltinge was an ingenue of a genie that once released could never be put back in the bottle—perfume, gin, or otherwise.

Little is known of his personal life, and by all accounts, he hid his sexuality from a speculative media. He built a magnificent home in Hollywood, the pink Villa Capistrano, where he lived with his dogs and his mother. Insert stereotypical rumors here. But beyond this, there is silence . . . and not just in film. The tabloids had him engaged to countless starlets, and he loved to toy with the press. Once, to prove his manhood, he staged a boxing match with "Gentleman Jim" Corbett. By most accounts, it was a draw . . . most probably of attention.

Perhaps not so curiously, he often found himself in innumerable fistfights with both stagehands and drunken cabaret patrons, ever demanding that his masculinity remain unquestioned. However, it was hard to pull this off when his stage monikers ranged from the "Crinoline Girl" to "Mr. Lillian Russell." He must have given his ever-struggling press agent quite the ulcer.

An impossible persona to typecast, Eltinge's greatest gift was perhaps his ability to not merely play a woman with complete believability but to also convincingly become one, which is why audiences claimed he was one of the greatest living actresses of his time. For Eltinge, it wasn't so much an act as a metamorphosis.

Today, Eltinge's influence on the twenty-first century is all around us, though you have to squint though some rather thick false eyelashes to see the cross-dressing ghosts.

Do you remember Julie Andrews's final wig reveal in *Victor/Victoria?* Not only did Eltinge invent that signature move, he virtually trademarked it throughout his career—and not at some drag bar but through a long and notable vaudeville career and concert appearances around the world.

There are numerous references to the Eltinge Theatre in Douglas Carter Beane's play *The Nance*. Though the theatre itself was a legitimate vaudeville house, by 1939 it had slipped into its darker (see: seedier) burlesque days. Mayor LaGuardia did his best to shut it down or at least limit the activities of single men in the darkened upper balconies.

"Alex, may I have 'Actors who played both male and female parts in the same play or film for one hundred?'" Um, Charles Ludlum, followed by Charles Busch, Dustin Hoffman, followed by . . . whom? It's a short list. Eltinge, on the other long glove, simultaneously played both sex roles so realistically that audiences often thought he had a body double. Yet if this was the one masterful trick of his career, it was an incomparable one.

Female impersonators such as Charles Pierce would later channel the star stylings of Mae West, Bette Davis, Tallulah Bankhead, the list is endless—yet that was not Eltinge. He was not a female impersonator in the classic sense but rather played characters as an actress; he was an actor playing a woman who just happened to be him/herself. In a fashion, Eltinge set the stage for the most famous male drag actor of the twentieth century: Harris Glenn Milstead, aka "Divine." Still, the great distinction is that Divine played it all for comic effect, whereas Eltinge was, mostly, coquettishly serious. In his silent pictures, title cards often revealed the laugh with barely an eye roll from Eltinge.

Eltinge's final performance was at Billy Rose's Diamond Horseshoe nightclub in New York City in February 1941. He died ten days later at his apartment on West 74th Street. His death, like much of his personal life, remains a mystery, leaving behind a bustle full of questions and, undoubtedly, many spectacular black veils.

CHAPTER 25

MARVIN: UNREAD

Marvin had spent the better part of the weekend dealing with crap.

Crap from the estate executor. who mercilessly prodded him into emptying a hoarder's house in an unreasonably tight time frame and an even tighter (see: cheap) budget.

Crap from the prissy realtor who held his nose up higher than the home's rising stench as he tiptoed through the rooms of trash in his Louis Vuitton shoes, demanding a spotlessly clean home for a near-immediate showing.

And finally, he dug actual dog crap out of this house by the hundreds of shovelfuls, the basement having been used as a pit bull breeding den.

Yes, the weekend was an absolute crap fest, yet Marvin still loved the work. It was his job, his company, and his workers, and few did it better. It wasn't lost on him that in his line of work, crap was an actual cash cow.

Now, at the end of the day, Marvin pulls into a snarl of traffic and takes what he thinks will be a shortcut home, but no luck; his long day stretches further than his patience.

He sits in his pickup truck, motionless on the highway, a light rain sprinkling down. There seems to be an accident ahead or, perhaps, too many idiots out late on a Friday night. Either way, he's stuck. The truck's cab reeks a noxious odor, and he knows he is the cause. The dog-crap-filled hoarder's house he'd just finished cleaning out now permeates his clothes, his hair, and his skin—seemingly into his bones. Mixed with his own sweat, the stench splays from his body like a silent, pungent explosion. All he can do is roll down the truck windows and try to catch a breath of something other than himself.

On the passenger seat beside him sits the book he'd so curiously discovered at the cleanout. If it smells, he can't tell. Probably doesn't matter.

Oddly, the book seems comforting, as if he had rescued a kitten from a storm drain in an act of kindness. Clearly, it's just an old book with some odd tales that, given a cursory glance, he can't quite figure out. All he knows is that he can't wait to tell his wife about the day's vile adventures and this one simple treasure he's claimed for his own.

As the rain comes down harder, Marvin rolls the truck's windows back up and endures his own foul-smelling self. The windshield wipers whack a rubbery back and forth; as the water comes down faster, the traffic now seems to move even slower. Every time he takes his foot off the brake to reach for the book, the traffic creeps ahead by a few feet, forcing him to put both hands back on the steering wheel. He's tired, and this is no time to be rereading peculiar passages from some old book. Only when the headlights of his truck finally flash on his own garage door can he relax.

"Marvin, you home?" comes Lorraine's voice from the kitchen. "Dinner's almost ready."

"Yup. I'm gonna take a quick shower." He sits the tattered book beside the front door, reminding himself to wipe it down later. A little water isn't going to ruin it after everything it's been through.

Lorraine pokes her head into the living room, frying pan in hand. "Hope you're hungry for pork chops, and I'm caramelizing those green peppers you like."

Marvin starts to peel off his clothes. "Perfect!" He grunts.

She pulls her head back into the kitchen doorway, her face tightening in a grimace. "Oh, lord. Is that you? Did something die?"

"What? Oh, the smell. Yeah, just my soul. The usual."

"No," she corrects, "it's way worse than usual. You're toxic. What did you clean out today, the morgue?"

Marvin laughs. "More like the Kennel Club."

Her voice trails back from the kitchen. "Now don't put those dirty clothes with the regular laundry. I hate when you do that." She pauses, then even louder: "Do you hear me?"

"Yes, yes!" Marvin tosses his clothes on the bathroom floor and climbs into a tepid shower, impatiently waiting for the hot water to arise from the basement. He trembles as the dirt starts to fall away from his body and the water's temperature increases to steam worthy. Now he can feel how badly his muscles ache, the soreness of a thousand shovel-filled stretches pulling his body apart. It's as if he'd started to dig a hole to China only to realize that digging sideways would never get him there.

As he pulls on clean jeans and a T-shirt, he can smell the grill of pork chops and peppers, a heavenly scent long overdue from the nastiness of the day. He only hopes Lorraine has made enough to satisfy his growling empty stomach.

"Another tough one?" asks Lorraine as she sets a piled-high plate in front of him.

He dives into the meal as if it were his last. "I've seen worse," he mumbles between bites, "but nothing quite as weird."

Lorraine pours each of them a glass of red wine. "Do tell, love. I'm all ears."

"So," he begins in mid-chew, "it wasn't exactly a hoarder's situation—worse really, but some poor old lady let these homeless guys into her house, and they turned it into a pit bull puppy mill."

She cuts into her meat. "Okay, now that's disgusting."

"Well, we're eating so I'm not gonna say how bad it was."

"Bad? I could smell you from the driveway!"

Marvin pulls a bit back from the table. "Still?"

"No, babe, you're fine, my handsome man. Eat." Lorraine stands to get him another pork chop. "You find anything good?"

Marvin has now polished off half his plate, leaving room for the next portion. "Almost nothing. It was bad. The college kids I hired were great, though, and helped me dig out all the trash from the basement. They worked like slaves. We really killed ourselves today."

Lorraine sips her wine and watches her husband gobble down the second chop. "Too bad you didn't find anything. We could use the extra cash. Today was a slow death at the salon. Literally. Old Mrs. Contorno never showed for her two o'clock appointment. Turns out she croaked last night."

"Heart attack?" Marvin guesses.

"Nah! Apparently, she threw a box of bagels at her daughter-in-law in a snit, fell backward, and broke her neck on a piano bench."

Marvin drops his fork. "Oh my god. That's terrible."

"The daughter-in-law feels terrible about it, of course," Lorraine explains. "Mrs. Contorno wanted jelly-filled donuts. Hated bagels. Everybody knew that. Heck, even I knew that."

Shaking his head, Marvin scrapes up the last of the caramelized peppers with his knife. "Are we sending flowers?"

"Nah!" Lorraine echoes once again. "The girls in the salon said we should send a carton of Marlboros to the American Cancer Society. Mrs. Contorno lived on Marlboros, coffee, and jelly donuts."

"Jeez!" Marvin scoffs. "Kind of dark, huh?

"It's a dark salon." She begins clearing the table but returns to the original question. "So, you find *anything* today we can turn into cash money? The only green we've had lately were these peppers."

"Well," Marvin starts with a hesitant drawl, "this might sound kind of crazy, but I did bring this one thing home." Wiping his mouth with the napkin, he bounds from the table.

Lorraine almost chokes on her pork chop bone. "You brought home something from that pit bull party house? Oh, I just had the carpeting cleaned."

Marvin runs back into the living room to retrieve the book. He can still hear Lorraine's admonishments from two rooms away as he takes the book into the bathroom to give it the once-over with a damp cloth.

"For god's sake, come back here and finish your dinner. You're acting crazy."

Returning to the dining room with book in hand, he nearly sits it on the table when Lorraine let out: "No, no, no!"

Marvin stops abruptly, now holding the book to his pounding chest. "Okay," he excitedly starts again. "This is crazy, the craziest thing ever. See, we'd cleaned out the entire house. Empty, Lorraine. I'm telling you, empty. Swept clean, debris free, nothing left. But when I did my final walk-through, this book was sitting in the middle of the bedroom floor."

Lorraine, holding a fork above a pork chop, simply glares at him. "A book? You're in a frenzy about some dirty old book?"

"Yes—well, no, not just a book. You had to be there. I'm telling you, it came out of nowhere. I mean, one minute it wasn't there, the next minute it was. Nobody else in the house but me."

"I think you need another glass of wine," decides Lorraine, pouring for them both.

"And the stories inside . . ." he continues. "I don't know if it's some type of crazy memoir or . . . well, sorta, kinda."

"I don't understand," she says with a shake of her head, "but I do know you'd better not sit that filthy thing down anywhere in my house."

Marvin hesitates for a moment then carefully places the book on the kitchen countertop.

Lorraine barks, "Not on the counter! That's even worse!"

He sits back down at the dinner table and takes a few gulps of wine, trying to relax. "I'm sorry. I'll disinfect it later. I'm exhausted!"

Lorraine moves to touch Marvin but then pulls back. "You should really wash your hands again."

"I'm fine," he says, returning to the last of his plate's scrapings. "It's just the oddest thing, and I can't explain it."

Lorraine pushes her dinner plate aside and reaches for her wine glass. "The book?"

"Yes, the book. What it says. How I found it. It's all really weird."

She rises from the dinner table, opens a kitchen cabinet drawer, and carefully places a pair of rubber gloves on her hands. Marvin, his back to her now, sips his wine in silence as she begins to examine the book. "So it's some artist's sketchbook . . . or what?"

"Sketchbook?" Marvin laughs, turning around in his seat to face her. "You see drawings? I didn't see any drawings."

She casually flips through the crumbling pages. "I don't see anything, Marvin. No words. No drawings. No nothing. It's blank."

"No, no. They're stories." Marvin grabs the book from her rubbery hands. He closes the book firmly then opens it again, as if attempting some odd magic trick that only he can perform.

He stares near hypnotically at the first page. It's blank. Then he turns to the second page. Blank. The third. All blank.

Marvin thrust the book out at arm's length and turns it upside down, shaking its spine as violently as he himself now shakes. He drops it to the floor and staggers back, confused and shuddering in his work-worn skin, silent in an inexplicable fear.

Lorraine pulls off her rubber gloves with a thwack and places her arms around her trembling husband. "Honey," she says softly, "don't bring home any more shit from work."

CHAPTER 26

RETAIL LOSES WAG; RESALE FINDS SWAG

On the near northwest side of Chicago at the long-venerated Six Corners business district stands an enormous, vacant Sears store: a historic empty flagship location for both for a lost brand and the adjacent neighborhood located at the intersection of three high-traffic streets.

Like the spokes of a once-loved but now broken bicycle, empty storefronts splay down each avenue in the hub, and dead retail stretches out in cursory, if not curious, ways. While some shop windows appear to be freshly vacated, others are painted over or boarded up or have transitioned into a strange hybrid of both. Is a new store opening, or has an old store just closed? Sadly, it is more often the latter.

Barely two miles to the west limps the Harlem Irving Plaza, commonly referred to as "the HIP." The remodeled indoor shopping mall was once anchored by the legendary Wieboldt's and Carson Pirie Scott & Co. (aka Carson's) department stores. The cavernous, empty first-floor space is now a hobby in search of a lobby.

The closings of the two retail behemoths, Sears and Carson's, were as dissimilar as they were uncomfortably familiar. At the Sears location, the long lines of final customers owed as much to the 70 percent off gold and silver jewelry as to the dearth of available cashiers. Yet the 10 to 20 percent discount offerings in virtually every other department reflected a retailer empty of values: not merely undiscovered but unwanted. In its death spiral, this Sears location proved staler than the preceding decades of decline: threadbare carpeting, broken linoleum, and inventory that, if not dated, surely wouldn't get a swipe on Retail Tinder.

Carson's, to its credit, had presented itself like an impressively sinking Titanic: majestic, sleek, and polished. The endcap displays sparkled with the seductive models of Calvin Klein, Michael Kors, and Anne Klein, all while careening toward an iceberg of impending insolvency. Unlike Sears, Carson's had a few brief months to sail those impossible waters, yet with only 20 percent off on everything (extra 10 percent on sleepy Mondays), the store had been a retail ghost town. Stylish teenage boys sampled cologne testers in the men's department, fingered $118 shirts, and then scratched their fresh haircuts as they attempted to calculate the discount.

Such is the state of retail across this city and the Walmart-bloated country from coast to coast. Still, there's something ominous about these particular Chicago-based closings. Chicago, dubbed "City on the Make" by author Nelson Algren, was infamous for legendary payoffs and politically infused payrolls, and it should have seen this coming. We all should have seen this coming. Such nostalgic shopping destinations were always more than mere neighborhood department stores; they were the anchors of the neighborhoods themselves, hosting shoppers as residents to these town squares of retail. But, as in life, retail changed.

Historically, Chicago's central location made it the perfect crossroad for the railroads and the commerce they would bring. While Sears and Montgomery Ward would reinvent the catalog business by bringing reasonably priced products to the doorways of middle America, upscale stores, such as Marshall Field's, entertained the monied upscale masses with merchandising that seemed more like great theatre. When Marshall Field so famously quoted: "Give the lady what she wants!" he meant it literally. Unsurpassed quality, free delivery, and an unquestioned return policy. In fact, customers were known to return items some twenty years after purchase, a policy Sears would later attempt to employ to a near-fatal retail effect.

The 120-year-old Bon-Ton department store chain and owner of the now-defunct Carson's joins other famous merchants—such as Toys "R" Us, Nine West, Claire's, and too many others to mention—in bankruptcy. And much like those early Chicago pioneers, all that mattered in the end was the land. No, modern merchants didn't need to scare off any Native Americans this time; the internet and—predominantly and carnivorously—Amazon took care of that.

But this is merely past as prologue. There's an odd twist in the retail air . . . and it's resale. Yes, that lazy, slow-moving, hard-to-define retail sector is estimated to be more than a $17 billion annual business, much of it generated from antiques/vintage stores and auction houses. But while most people think of resale as charity thrifts and secondhand stores—an accurate description if you're defining a down-low market—you'd be remiss if you didn't notice the bigger picture developing—and not just in Chicago.

Like the little collectibles engine that could, websites like eBay, Etsy, Chairish, Mercari, Ruby Lane, and the high-end noses of the RealReal and 1stdibs are established players in the business of online resale. And for all the privacy infractions Americans have recently endured, it hasn't stopped hundreds of thousands of resellers from posting their wares on Facebook Marketplace and Craigslist, creating a new generation of mom-and-pop businesses. Further, design-savvy sites like Instagram and TikTok have created cyber sellers who collect followers like a poker player counting cards.

In the end, it's a numbers game, and resale finally appears to be a significantly valuable part of the American economy, morphing from a metaphorical Six Corners to one corner of your home office in your basement or garage. It is common for resellers to rent storage lockers for additional inventory and/or showroom space. And yes, those questionable storage-locker-auction reality shows (fake or real) have brought the resale business to a complete, if not dizzying, circle.

While the cancer of American retail has metastasized into a slow going-out-of-business death, resale has been steadily growing in collectible fits and categorized niches. Some trends, like the reemerging interest in vintage vinyl, have been game changers. New brick-and-mortar record stores are popping up everywhere, a concept few could have predicted a short decade ago. Record Store Day (April 21) routinely sets higher yearly benchmarks with thousands of new and vintage retailers posting record-setting sales.

Vintage clothing has also exploded for a myriad of reasons: the quality of vintage fabrics and a new appreciation for past fashions plus the murky trend of new designers knocking off old designs are making the originals more desirable and often more affordable. So, if you want to show some serious glam—and be environmentally savvy to boot—the catwalk is vintage green.

We must also include mass media: cable outlets, such as Netflix, Hulu, and countless others, have had a significant effect on resale. Today, there is rarely a film/television production or commercial that doesn't reflect the visual vintage vibe. And that didn't happen overnight . . .

From the first few episodes of *Mad Men*, a renaissance of mid-century modern nearly everything began to sweep the country. Suddenly, your Aunt Lola's "'50s crap" was now the backdrop of America's latest design-centric soap opera. The fashions may have been at the forefront, but so were those never-ending cocktail hours, the retro shakers similarly stirred, and many a mid-mod casting couch. Don Draper's sexy suited self may have seduced many a vintage-clad vixen, yet it was America that fell in love/lust with its formerly stylish self. Vintage was no longer *yesterday*; it was tomorrow's look and often for less.

Consider Hollywood's influence. Noted collector, historian, and producer of the World's Fair Memorabilia Show, Rick Rann, says: "Since the 2003 publication of the book *The Devil in the White City* by Erik Larson, a true-crime drama centered near the 1893 Chicago World's

Fair, Hollywood has had this film in development. That book introduced the 1893 Chicago Exposition to many young people, and there are many more '1893 collectors' than there were twenty years ago." Perhaps unsurprisingly, the anticipation of the film alone seems to have influenced the resale marketplace. In fact, as of early 2022, Keanu Reeves is now set to star in a limited series about that first American serial killer, H. H. Holmes, for Hulu. Look for increased sales after *The Devil in the White City* airs!

Strengthened by the Chicago connection, renewed interest in objects and ephemera from the 1933 Century of Progress International Exposition has been sparked as well. Continues Rann: "Our shows have seen a 20 percent increase in exhibitors over previous years, most dealers saying they've had solid shows with strong year-over-year sales. Attendance is up; interest is up; everything is on the upswing."

Other vintage-memorabilia show promoters echo similar trends across the resale spectrum, experiencing significantly greater attendance to their venues and bottom-line profitability. Says Sally Schwartz, producer of Chicago's legendary Randolph Street Market: "What we are seeing is the young affluent demo are all about vintage lifestyle in their home decor and wearables. They want to feel 'organic' and embrace recycling, and they are suspicious and wary of mass marketing, sweatshop labor, etc. They like to feel unique, and resale finds are random and surprising and often one of a kind."

Suddenly, this underground economy is no longer under anything except perhaps underrated expectations. For years, the public has viewed retail and resale as two distinctly different marketplaces. Now, with the maturing of the internet, resale has cleaned up its act, evolving, if not rebranding, itself as the "retail of resale." At first glance, that may appear too fine a point, but for those who understand, it's one mighty profitable distinction.

Finally, consider that resale is a "one-off" business model for the most part and is not easily replicated by the likes of Jeff Bezos. If we're lucky, he'll keep his eyes on the stars, leaving the rest of us to market our Star Wars collectibles one Wookie at a time.

While the big-brand landscape falters and retail supply chain troubles clog up the economy like a thickening artery, the resale/retailing universe continues to expand and profit parallel to the public's growing interest in all things vintage.

So may the resale force be with us all. It's not as if the cosmos will be running out of vintage stuff any day soon. Resale be yanking that supply chain, baby! The future is yesterday . . .

Update: Two of the intersecting Six Corners streets have been developed into luxury apartment complexes.

With windows punched into the enormous blank façade of the old Sears store and new construction flanking its opposite corner, life has returned in the form of residential units with upscale amenities. The retail streetscape scene now offered is a drastically downscaled version from the historic nature of this famous Chicago shopping district. By destiny, if not geography itself, there will always be Six Corners. However, like an outdated six-cornered hat, fashion will most assuredly follow this style dysfunction.

CHAPTER 27

WONDERS OF THE WORLD THAT NEVER WERE

Most people are content to fulfill their personal interests with "What's new?" or "What's different?" Oddly, I am interested in "What isn't" or more correctly, "What wasn't"—that which has not been fulfilled or fully realized.

Nothing bothers me more than being promised something and then not getting it. Maybe it goes back to some childhood memory of a disappointing Christmas where my spoiled self felt promised something and then an adult backed out of the deal. You know who you are, Uncle "Where's my hovercraft?"

In the spirit of the late drag actor Divine screaming, "I wanted cha-cha heels!" I offer the following: Wonders of the World That Never Were. Five big things on my wish list of wonderful that never came to pass . . . like a promised kidney stone.

Personally, I feel cheated, and you should too.

THE CHICAGO SPIRE

Cancelled skyscrapers are nothing new in America or throughout the world. However, Chicago has a long and famous architectural history with projects that never got off the ground. Literally. Very few A-list architects become famous without first designing something notable in Chicago. This has been true ever since an allegedly impatient cow in need of milking kicked Mrs. O'Leary's flame and fortune into the future. That cow cleared a lot of land for Frank Gehry, I'll tell you that. Though the story has since been disproven and Irish Chicagoans ostracized for many a year, it didn't stop them from exacting their revenge via the Daley dynasty and giving the world tripe: cow stomach cooked with milk and onions. (Yes, this is how the Chicago River is turned green on every St. Patty's Day!) But I digestively digress . . .

The Chicago Spire was a dream project. In the end, that's all it was, but for a brief moment in time, it was a dream in a starring role. Conceived as one of the tallest buildings in America at 2,000 feet and 150 floors, the structure had everything going for it: a famous architect, Santiago Calatrava, and an incredible location a few hundred feet from Chicago's tourist-crazy Navy Pier and lakefront. Plus, it was an architectural design worthy of awe. But perhaps the Chicago Spire was never truly inspired by more than making a fast buck.

In 2007, the project was approved by the Chicago City Council faster than any proposal in the city's history. And do you know how many aldermen have construction companies with their own projects in the works? Plenty. Being an alderman is a part-time job, so they all have extra time to buy property, run hot dog stands, shake down unlicensed eyebrow threading trucks, etc. All important things, no doubt. Still, all this was put aside to push through the approval of this massive skyscraper. Back then, what Major Daley wanted, Mayor Daley got.

Nelsen Algren's cross-dressing nephew was right: it is the City of Big Shoulder Pads . . .

When the bottom (and in this case, also the top) of the real estate market dropped out, it was over. Though the Spire's developers were able to secure leases for the bottom floors of the structure with retail, multiplexes, and multi-Starbucks locations, the hundreds of condominiums above remained unsold and a hotel undeveloped.

Except for the top penthouse (141st and 142nd floors) purchased by Ty Warner, creator of the Beanie Baby, the middle of the building somehow went missing . . . no condo buyers, no hotel. Warner's 10,000-square-foot duplex was listed at $40 million, but the final sales price was never disclosed. Given the building's ultimate demise, I'm certain his deposit was returned—Aldi the Alcoholic Alderman Antelope having an exceptional lawyer.

After the hotel concept was scrapped, all that was left were the promises of unsold apartments between the retail development on the bottom floors and Kingdom of Beanies above. Oh, and stuffings of lawsuits in between—lots and lots of lawsuits.

For many years, all that remained was a very large and unusual circular hole in the ground. When it rained, the hole filled with plenty of room for Seamore Seal and his Beanie friends to flounder in the glory of what wasn't.

THE TITANIC HOTEL

There's bad taste—and then there's the Titanic Hotel, Las Vegas. This recreation of the fated luxury liner *RMS Titanic* was to be a themed resort and hotel boasting some twelve hundred rooms. Scale, as you know, is everything in Vegas—be it a cup sized for your quarters or your bosoms—and this development was no different.

Measuring approximately four hundred feet high—twice that of the original ship—it was to be constructed across from the Sahara hotel and casino at a cost of some $1.2 billion dollars.

Though the project was eventually nixed by the Las Vegas City Council (imagine the sinking ship-themed simulator ride!), the website is still surprisingly up at titanicresort.com. Check it out for some amazingly cheesy graphics and every ice reference to be found in your frozen thesaurus. In addition to the standard Las Vegas fare, the hotel was to feature a petting zoo . . . cuz you know how much killer whales love to be petted by the broke and inebriated.

I can't imagine what the marketing people had in mind with this concept: "Gamble with your money, not your life"? It makes that Dead Sea Carnival Cruise look most appealing.

PEE-WEE LAND

This is a story that is perhaps more urban myth fiction than reality fact, but I'm telling it anyway.

At the height of Pee-wee Herman's fame and fortune, the boy in the ill-fitting suit had the world on its knees, a position Miss Yvonne was not always unfamiliar with. In addition to the Pee-wee's Playhouse franchise and the phenomenal success of a young Tim Burton's *Pee-wee's Big Adventure*, this little P. W. was making huge bucks.

At the zenith of his frenzy, Herman had yearly merchandising sales in excess of $25 million, mostly from toys. Yet in the works were many things, including a line of kids' clothes at JCPenney, a breakfast cereal, and yes, as mentioned in *People* magazine in 1989, his own amusement park. "A warped version of Disneyland," he predicted at the time.

Though people were throwing land at him like magic words (*"bukkake"*) the rumor mill whispered Pee-wee was buying up property in Hollywood under assumed names (Constance Amnesia, Placenta Flambé, Chastity Stirrup, etc.) in and around where the Dolby Theatre now stands. I have not been able to locate the photo—I saw it only once and cannot verify its authenticity—but the property had been fenced off and a sign posted: "Coming Soon . . . Pee-wee Land!"

Sadly, when Pee-wee's little slacks hit the floor, so did Pee-wee Land. Captain Carl and Cowboy Curtis were replaced by two vice detectives in that now infamous LA porn theatre raid. Yes, Pee-wee came THIS close to relaunching a West Coast Village People.

The rest, as they say, is his story. Not that anyone believed it. Did the media, the public, and his toked-out adult fans overreact? In hindsight, perhaps. He seems a fine man, a funny actor, and he created a character that will live forever. Rather like Chaplin's Little Tramp, except Pee-wee's white loafers tended to stick.

The same cannot be said for Pee-wee Land. Was it just a dream on paper? Just a fib Pee-wee told? And could not the psychically disembodied Jambi have given Pee-wee a heads-up? Of course, no one ever wants bad news. Especially on a pink Princess telephone.

Now, we can only imagine what wondrous rides would have been inspired by the original Playhouse and the fun we would have had. "Woulda, coulda, shoulda!" Right, Pee-wee?

"What's today's secret word?" Disappointed.

SUNSET BOULEVARD: THE MOVIE MUSICAL

"But wait," you say, "this is happening!" Um, perhaps/maybe. This on-again, off-again movie musicalization of Andrew Lloyd Webber's Hollywood opera has been stop-lighted so often, it's enough to make you want to shoot anyone seeking a midnight swim.

Rumor reads that Glenn Close has snagged the role of the tragic Norma Desmond, but you know Meryl Streep can play anything, including that dead monkey part in cameo. Barbra Streisand's name was floated about for a time, but then she wants to direct. And Cecil B. DeMille—sorry Andrew Lloyd Webber—would never hear of it.

And then there was that ancient story about Andrew L. W. offering the part to Madonna, but she wasn't about to play someone THAT old. Don't cry for me, Argentina. Or 10086 Sunset Boulevard, for that matter.

That's the downside of creating a diva: you give and you give, yet still it's hard to fill those big heels and bigger egos. This is not the first time Sir Andrew has created a monster; the movie version of Phantom made a big *PLOP* sound in both the river beneath the opera house and at a theatre near you. And don't you dare ask about Phantom's sequel, *Love Never Dies* . . . or as they jest in the trade, *Paint Never Dries.*

My personal casting remains: Glenn Close as Norma Desmond (eccentric/crazy); Channing Tatum as Joe (stud puppet paradise); Patrick Stewart as Max (elegant and faded sexy). And as for the monkey, I'm sure Zach Galifianakis is available, and they'll save a fortune on costuming.

HANDCARVED COFFINS: THE FILM

Originally published in Andy Warhol's *Interview* magazine and later in *Music for Chameleons, Truman Capote's Handcarved Coffins: A Non Fiction Account of an American Crime* is second only to *In Cold Blood* for the genius of the conceit, if not the writing. Returning to his "nonfiction novel" format, Capote places himself in this intriguing tale of a serial killer but with a twist: before their cleverly devised deaths, each victim receives an exquisitely made miniature handcarved coffin with their own tiny photo inside. Chills!

The premise: A detective investigating the case falls in love (of course) with a soon-to-be victim. He must solve the case before she, too, is killed in a mostly grisly way. Capote himself meets with the killer, but he may have met his match. Can he prove the killer's guilt or innocence? Could you be next? (Hint: don't accept any unwanted Amazon deliveries.)

According to author Steven Bach's book *Final Cut,* film rights to *Handcarved Coffins* were originally secured by United Artists for $250,000 just prior to their corporate sinking by the notorious Michael Cimino's budget-busting film *Heaven's Gate.* Hal Ashby had been slated to direct. Truman took the money and croaked in 1984, though not before United Artists hit the ground first. The studio 20th Century Fox would later pick up the option where the would-be film has floated about for years—most recently to the estate of Dino De Laurentiis.

Handcarved Coffins could very well be the greatest unresolved literary hoax of our time, but that's just another odd feature to this "sorta" true-crime puzzler. To this day, it remains one of the most unusual films never made.

Have a suggestion for more "Wonders of the World That Never Were"? Just let me know before I promise another book I have no intention of writing.

CHAPTER 28

THE SHATTERING

In the early morning hours just a few dizzy days before Christmas 2019, the angry ruckus of a cat fight erupted atop my aging refrigerator.

I didn't see it happen, but I heard that all-too-familiar crash of tchotchkes heading south, felines Mistacha and Buster being the likely suspects in the brawl. And though no fur was flung, big tails reluctantly greeted me with even greater surprise, each pointing blame at the other like children caught in a prank gone wrong.

On the kitchen floor lay the remains of a child's ceramic mug. At its base, the black words "Whistle for Your Milk" were barely visible, while across its relief had been a small embossed bear already missing both of its googly eyeballs, the lost off-kilter stare long gone.

The green handle of the mug once formed a tree branch, while a smaller three-dimensional bear rode its stem to the tip of the whistle spout. Marked "Made in Japan" on the bottom, I recall the year 1962 beside it in a circle, though I may have misremembered this due to advancing age and my losing love affair with better brands of vodka.

All was silent and still, like a crime scene waiting for the slow forensic reveal. Save for two kitties fast scampering into opposite rooms for inexcusable refuge, my kitchen floor was now splattered with a few dozen small shards of something that had once been wonderful.

My whistling-bear milk mug—inadvertently left atop the refrigerator long ago during a sorry attempt at cleaning/organizing—had suffered an unsurvivable fall. During any wild and unwinnable swatting of angry feline paws, few items ever successfully dodged the tumult of their ESPN-worthy battles. But the point, like the mug, was moot.

For those familiar with my first vintage memoir, *Selling Dead People's Things*, I made an early mention of my four-year-old self watching the lunchtime television broadcast of *Bozo's Circus* when the show was abruptly interrupted with news of the shooting of President Kennedy. "Who's he?" I ignorantly mumbled. You know the rest of the sad story.

On my menu that day was a PB&J sandwich and its requisite partner, cold white milk. Held tightly in my little hands was this particular "Whistle for Your Milk" bear mug. Until meeting its demise during the Mistacha/Buster Christmas brawl, I had all but forgotten about it.

Now I wondered whether it had forgotten about me as well.

As I moved from childhood into adulthood and to more "hoods" than I can remember—while all too frequently schlepping my possessions about in assorted boxes and bags—that little milk mug was packed and unpacked time and again with all the carelessness of a drunken mailman.

I had always been sloppy with my things, and this whistling-bear milk mug perpetually took the brunt of my inattentiveness. Its ending was an accident, assuredly due to my negligence, and the blame is self-evident. It's what I deserved for not being more thoughtful and careful and not appreciating something that had been with me for nearly sixty years, all the while it asking nothing in return but its safety. And now? Rest in pieces.

Some of you probably think this a special bit of kitty kat karma for a guy who wrote a book about the importance of collectible objects in people's lives. In this, you would not be mistaken. "People are their things," I've stated as the topic sentence in countless print, radio, and podcast interviews. "People are defined by what they collect and cherish." Yet what does it say when you lose a part of yourself, even if that fragment is a seemingly insignificant ceramic trifle?

In retrospect, the whistling-bear mug followed me through any number of love affairs and breakups and living single or with assorted roommates. It had even escaped two home robberies (in the same week) that left me with little more than the clothes on my back and a bear milk mug that whistled. Even thieves hadn't wanted it—and they'd carted off a ten-year-old microwave.

In the big picture, the loss of something as inconsequential as my whistling-bear milk mug seems near ridiculous, even silly. But I'd be remiss if I didn't admit that a tear or three was shed that morning as I scooped up the remaining shards and inexplicably placed them in a clear plastic bag for a reason I have yet to rationalize. I wasn't—and still am not—able to toss it out.

I was miserable most of the following day, but why? An object I hadn't used in nearly six decades was now beyond repair. Superglue couldn't fix the physical object or my mental state. Why did that bother me so much? Had a part of my childhood been lost? Could an old man's memories chip away so easily?

In the end, I suppose it's hard to brave the shallow waters of sentimentality, nostalgia, pathos, or even death without first drowning in a pool of one's own self-actualized clichés. Or as the poet Cher so aptly said with a face slap: "Snap out of it!"

Still, something critical happened over that Christmas, and it occurred not just to the whistling-bear milk mug and me; it would consume us all as well.

The year that followed was 2020, which would reveal unimaginable loss, most critically to humanity and to those we love and strangers alike, but also to our precious world. In the course of barely eighteen months, more Americans would die of COVID-19 than AIDS over some forty years.

Having somehow survived that first plague, I was no more prepared for the second—its virulence as viciously unfair and horrific. If anything, my fear was now magnified, as was the fear of nearly everyone who lived through the nightmare of those years. In the LGBTQ community alone, the better part of an entire generation was lost to AIDS.

Think about that.

No premonition was needed to see where we were all headed with COVID-19. An airborne plague, its ease of transmission fooled so many; some were woefully ignorant, others innocent yet still caught in the crosshairs of media lies and misinformation. The parallels between AIDS and COVID-19 are many, but the victim blaming/shaming was, and still is, nearly identical.

The finality of both plague stories will feature the forever-linked words: behavior, unfair, and cruel.

So often, life is simply taken for granted. When it goes well, it is glorious. Yet when one's health or the health of a loved one becomes dismantled, when we tumble and hit the ground hard, shattering into dozens of pieces and irreparably broken, we ask: "How did this happen? How did we fall so far, so fast?" And the inevitable: "Why?"

I'm going to go out on what's left of a ceramic limb here: Stop for a simple moment. Stop blaming yourself. Stop blaming one another. Stop blaming a political party. And stop blaming the cats.

Shatterings—and shat—happens.

Restart by treasuring yourself so you can treasure others. Cherish everything most fragile in your life. Secure what needs to be best secured: your health, your loved ones, your pets, and whatever seemingly silly little things in life you've held precious to this sliver of today.

In the end, you may very well find it's the whistle you don't hear that pitches the most memorable song.

CHAPTER 29

VOWS REJECTED

New York Times

SUNDAY STYLE SECTION, VOWS—JANUARY 2020

David Kensington, the son of Margaret and Richard Kensington of New Rochelle, New York, is to be married at Magnolia Bakery's original Bleecker Street location to Duane Scott Cerny, son of Gail and Lorraine Cerny of Chicago, Illinois, this Sunday, the 19th of January.

Mr. Kensington's family, though not originating from the Mayflower per se, descended directly from a long line of less-than-reputable dockworkers who assisted in the unloading of much of the Mayflower's missing luggage.

Mr. Cerny's lineage can be traced back to the 1871 Great Chicago Fire, when his great-great-grandmother lived "two doors down" from Mrs. O'Leary and her unfortunate livestock choices. It has been rumored the Cerny's donkey, Daisy, had a brief assignation with Mrs. O'Leary's cow, Mr. Lucky—hence the alleged kicking over of a lantern and the ensuing conflagration. Though DNA testing was unavailable at the time, this beefy/donkey genealogical stock has been historically documented at numerous drunken Midwest barbeques.

Messrs. Kensington and Cerny met atop the billiard table at the Eagle NYC, though strangely neither was using cue sticks at the time. Mr. Kensington, a well-known ophthalmologist whose work can be seen in the optical departments of better Walgreens' locations, first noticed Mr. Cerny while he was dominating the Eagle's resident bootblack over the correct polishing of his Prada fencing slippers.

Magnolia Bakery was chosen for the nuptials because it had a shorter line than the American Girl store at Rockefeller Center.

Update: Sadly, Mr. Kensington and Mr. Cerny broke up barely a year after their marriage, citing irreconcilable differences over nonstick cookware conflicts and a Grindr software glitch. (Sad emoticon!) Mr. Kensington, it should be noted, is more Williams-Sonoma, whereas Mr. Cerny is more Bed, Bath & Bear 411.

***

New York Times
SUNDAY STYLE SECTION, VOWS—JANUARY 2021
Kismet was in the air last November when Mr. Stuart Bartel, the son of highly rated Uber driver Hymie Bartel and Airbnb hostess Sadie Bartel, decided to relieve himself while awaiting the PATH subway train at the Christopher Street stop, Greenwich Village, New York City.

Only by love's coincidence was Mr. Cerny standing nearby and noticed Mr. Bartel's anatomical correctness suddenly being released into the transit air. Acting instinctively, Mr. Cerny provided a "reach around" to direct Mr. Bartel's urinary stream of unconsciousness away from the third rail, saving both his life and availability as a single man. Yes, in one stroke in that subway tunnel, love was found, a rat was drowned, and a happy ending was back on track. Well, except for the rat (see: NYT Obituaries, "Tony the Rat, Father of 15,000, Killed in Shocking PATH Accident").

Mr. Bartel is a well-regarded pet phrenologist and part-time cat masseuse who practices on the Upper East Side when his GPS is working correctly. His great-great-grandmother, Dame Sidney Phelmingdale Prunecastle-Cavalcade, is often referred to as the "face of modern-day syphilis," not because she imported the venereal disease from England but because she was just that damn ugly.

Mr. Cerny is a descendant of the obscure and often-mispronounced nineteenth-century composer Carl Czerny and routinely uses this ruse to secure better tables at lesser Chinese restaurants. Professionally, Mr. Cerny is an MCM antiques dealer and an off-season travel specialist for agoraphobics. In his spare time, he volunteers at Katy's House, which is a safe space for people of all nonbinary gender identifications to dispose of their Katy Perry CDs and memorabilia without shame or judging.

Messrs. Bartel and Cerny will be married at the Magnolia Bakery in the lower level of Grand Central Station, as long as Mr. Cerny's first husband (insolent diva David Kensington) doesn't show up and throw a hissy fit like he did at the closing drag party at Boots & Saddle.

Update: Sadly, due to an ugly disagreement over wedding invitation fonts and a misplaced phonetically impaired apostrophe, the Bartel/Cerny marriage was scrubbed after a few short months of one-sided counseling. For those interested, Mr. Bartel is available for further scrubbing at the West Side Club, room 307. Ask for Roberto. Venmo only, please.

***

New York Times
SUNDAY STYLE SECTION, VOWS—JANUARY 2022

It is often said, "The third time's a charm," but it was on a Gamblers Anonymous flight returning from Las Vegas where the dice of love was tossed. Duane Scott Cerny, son of Czechoslovakian glass bong blowers, bet everyone on the airplane that it "wouldn't crash" and made $300 from the wagering passengers.

Reginald Ward Plimpton III, son of Reginald Ward Plimpton II and Patricia Plath Plimpton, notable retailers of "Triple P" incontinency supplies, was immediately struck by both Mr. Cerny's clever scam and a removable tray table he used to obtain the money he won. The quick-thinking ice-pack actions of a handsome flight attendant saved the day, giving birth to both the duo's romance and an awkward pass at an abbreviated three-way.

Flying first class on another party's dime, the pair indulged in endless cocktails and multiple delicious kosher meals, eventually discovering their mutual obsession over reruns of *The Golden Girls,* notably the secret life of Bea Arthur and her rare appearance in the vilified 1978 *Star Wars Holiday Special.*

Speaking of keeping everything kosher, Mr. Plimpton acknowledged to Mr. Cerny that he was on PrEP (for HIV). However, Mr. Cerny, having had way too many complimentary gin and tonics, thought he'd said

"Preparation H." Thankfully, the two met safely in the medicated middle, and talk of an engagement was soon in the pressurized air.

Mr. Plimpton is a well-reviewed (see: Yelp, 3 stars!) cryogenic specialist who has frozen the heads of many late but semi-famous film and TV personalities, as well as less-notable parts of other industry members listed on IMDB.

Mr. Cerny made the bulk of his fortune in collectibles futures until the bottom dropped out of the vintage lunchbox market. Today, he sells character-themed thermos bottles on Etsy; Mrs. Beasley is his best seller.

The couple plans to be wed while waiting in line at Magnolia Bakery's Rockefeller Center location, barring any of Mr. Cerny's ex-husbands/fiancé's "frosting" the occasion for dietary, religious, or decorative design reasons.

Update: In the end, Mr. Cerny did not marry Mr. Plimpton. Unbeknownst to Mr. Cerny, those in the cryogenic field are often notoriously cold. Also, Mr. Plimpton being a stubborn, angry, and overly possessive Taurus didn't help matters. Mr. Cerny, it should be noted, is once again single and looking forward to walking down yet another aisle with his eyes set on the Magnolia Bakery in Bloomingdales but would also consider the express lane at Jenny Craig.

Editor's note:

1. The *New York Times* regrets the previous vows/ wedding announcements and, well, most everything else in the Sunday Style section.

2. Further, the paper regrets fawning over any film star taking a six-week Broadway stab in a drama, comedic play, or most notably, a musical.

3. In the event this book is turned into anything short of a doorstop, the *New York Times* retains the rights to speak glowingly about the author and the graciousness of its own good humor.

CHAPTER 30

QUOTE/ UNQUOTE

At Chicago's Broadway Antique Market (BAM), a mid-century modern store, our much beloved customer/ collector requests have evolved into something, well . . . rather unique.

"We receive dozens of these bizarre requests every week," explained store manager and graphic designer Eric Swanger to one of our non-believing dealers. "It's just part of the business. You can't make this stuff up. You begin think you've heard it all, and then you get verbally sideswiped. Wow, I didn't see that one coming! Now how do I answer that? Over time, I realized most of these requests fell into three categories: (1) confused/ mispronounced, (2) outlandish/bizarre, and/or (3) hands-down hilarious."

Eventually, these peculiar requests filtered up to my business partner, Jeff Nelson. Remembering one such inquiry, he further explained, "The gentleman who requested a clothing-optional night of antique shopping was completely serious. He claimed his group from California often shopped vintage stores 'in the nude' after hours. Apparently, they found it quite liberating, although I don't know where anyone kept their wallets. When the customer made this particular request, I was initially more concerned about our huge display windows that face a busy street; people seeing customers shopping naked seemed like a problem. Well, that and where people would sit? To be honest, I was equally worried about our vintage upholstery."

Seeing a trend, our employees started to compare notes, and an in-store contest was born: the Oddest Customer Request of the Week. The winning weird "ask" was rewarded with coffee from a nearby brew house . . . or pub, should the customer comment be particularly booze-worthy.

After collecting comments for over a year, I began editing out the offensive, inappropriate, and politically incorrect requests. To be clear, some things can be asked, but they should remain unfulfilled, unrepeatable, or at least unprintable. Designer Swanger, however, thought there was something more to the literary aberrations. He recalled seeing a postcard from a Michelin-rated

Chicago gastropub that used bad Yelp reviews in their advertising. That was his eureka design moment. What if he could turn these odd antiques requests into a promotional Christmas card? Could he turn crazy into festive?

Though skeptical at first, I soon warmed to the idea when I saw the first draft of the holiday greeting. I immediately liked the Scrabble or crossword puzzle element. It was a completely nontraditional holiday card, but it also reflected the way we communicate today, the use of social media, and the explosion of the tweet. More importantly, I thought the card was honest. Every request is a true comment, every phrase a short story. See—you can't make this shit up!

Here is a portion of the original—and still rather lengthy—customer comment list assembled by the staff for our holiday promotion:

- What do all these *Sold* tags mean?
- I'm looking for something shaped like a brick.
- Why aren't all your earrings cufflinks?
- Why aren't all your cufflinks earrings?
- Where are your vintage bongs, man?
- I'm looking for something I don't think was ever made.
- Will things be cheaper when you go out of business?

- Is that like a famous mirror?
- Do you get all this stuff from a catalog?
- Is this like a museum, or isn't anything for sale?
- I'm selling a coffin that was only used once.
- I don't want an appraisal; I just want to know what it's worth.
- Can you recommend another store that won't buy my things?
- How much is free shipping?
- What's the least you'll take for something I'm not buying today?
- When you say "pair," how many is that?
- I'm looking for something that I think is illegal to sell.
- Do famous rabbis ever shop here?
- Have you ever sold a repossessed Ouija board?
- Can my dog shop here? Sometimes he bites children.
- What's your return policy on something I just broke?
- How old does something have to be before it's worthless?
- Can I return something I didn't buy here?
- What's the least you'll take for an item marked

"not for sale"?

- Just so you know: you're not as famous as people say you are.

- My mom's having an estate sale, but she doesn't know about it yet.

- I'm thinking of starting a clock collection, but I don't have time to shop today.

- Why are your paperweights so heavy?

- Why are your vintage clothes so small? Weren't there any fat people years ago?

- Except for the prices, what's the difference between a thrift store and an antiques store?

- I was here five years ago, and you had something purple.

- What's your number-one selling item that I can buy and resell for more money?

- What's your favorite thing in the store that won't sell?

- How long does an item have to be here before it's free?

- Have you ever caught people having sex in the dressing room?

- How fast can you sell something?

- I'll be doing a lingerie photo shoot here next weekend, so you know.
- I'm selling one hundred thousand condoms, most of them mint in the box.
- I need cheap suits of armor . . . and fast.
- I was here years ago before this place was built.
- So . . . a half dozen is five, right?
- Do I have to feed the parking meter if I'm not shopping?
- So you know, there are people having sex in your alley . . . and they don't like me watching.

Quotes Update:
After more than twenty years in vintage retailing at the Broadway Antique Market, we thought we'd heard it all. Apparently not. Today, the curious customer comments and/or requests continue to flow into our ready ears, if not our hard-to-shock composures.

Example
Customer: "I don't need to wear a mask. I'm from Kansas."

Reply: "You're not in Kansas anymore, Dorothy! Put on your goddamn mask."

While finishing this book, I realized that perhaps the

business of resale fosters thoughts that would otherwise be left unsaid; vintage is an emotional, memory-based industry that can prompt subconscious ideas to be verbalized via the little voice in your head that normally keeps its trap shut.

Why do we ask so many questions of others yet are unwilling to answer the more indelicate questions of ourselves? My best guess is that truth is one tenacious bitch. Or as an employee once said after a particularly disastrous resale incident: "I wasn't there that day! (Long pause) Now, what day *was* it again?"

Possibly you have some questions of your own. Or perhaps you can see parts of yourself within some of these *Vintage Confidential* tales. If so, let me get my note-book . . .

If not, maybe I best mind my own business. Literally. Stop by and see us if you're in the neighborhood or check out the website www.bamchicago.com for more MCM delights. And if you haven't already read *Selling Dead People's Things* yet, it's on Amazon and better indie bookstores. Enjoy!

IS THIS THE PLACE PEOPLE TOLD ME ABOUT? WHAT DO ALL THESE SOLD TAGS MEAN? I'M LOOKING FOR SOMETHING SHAPED LIKE A BRICK. ARE YOU EVER OPEN WHEN YOU'RE NOT OPEN? WHY AREN'T ALL YOUR EARRINGS CUFFLINKS? WHERE ARE YOUR VINTAGE BONGS, MAN? I'M LOOKING FOR SOMETHING I DON'T THINK WAS EVER MADE. WILL THINGS BE CHEAPER IF YOU GO OUT OF BUSINESS? YOU SHOULD HAVE A CLOTHING OPTIONAL NIGHT. IS THAT LIKE A FAMOUS MIRROR? DO YOU GET ALL THIS STUFF FROM A CATALOG? IF I DON'T SEE WHAT I WANT IS IT SOMEPLACE ELSE? IS THIS LIKE A MUSEUM OR ISN'T ANYTHING FOR SALE? IF I DON'T BUY THIS WILL SOMEONE ELSE? BAM

ACKNOWLEDGMENTS

I WISH TO THANK:

My partner, Jeff Nelson, for his support and encouragement

BAM Manager Eric Swanger, designer of the holiday artwork insert

Editor Jill Welsh for her wise word-by-word guidance

Copyeditor Kim Bookless for her detailed mindfulness

Japanese translator Saeko Goto Thompson for her corrective accuracy

Cover designer Gwyn Flowers of GKS Creative for her patience

Bethany Brown and The Cadence Group team for knocking this out of the proverbial production park

Gretchen Cryer, Julie Gold, Brad Forenza, Boze Hadleigh, Sally Schwartz, Chip Cordelli, Brenda Currin, Melissa Sands, and Mark Contorno for their kind words

Sarese Hranicka, who encouraged many an antiques store to carry my books, spreading the gospel of vintage by any means necessary

The many independent bookstores across the country that have kept brick-and-mortar retail alive and reading

My vintage-obsessed fans who not only enjoy my books . . . but also enjoy reselling them!

ABOUT THE AUTHOR

DUANE SCOTT CERNY is co-owner of the Broadway Antique Market, Chicago's oldest and largest multi-dealer vintage shopping destination. The author's first book, *Selling Dead People's Things*, is a memoir of his exploits in the antiques world. It was excerpted in the *New York Times* and named one of the Top 20 Memoirs of the Year by The Advocate, and it went on to become an Amazon #1 Best Seller. Cerny has appeared on over two hundred TV, radio, and podcast interviews, as well as in the dreams of the disappointed. He resides in Chicago and New York City's Greenwich Village but someday hopes to live in the Metaverse where he will be younger, richer, smarter, better looking, and much, much taller.

For book orders, fan/hate mail, or holographic personal appearance requests, please visit:

www.VintageConfidential.com